James

THE STEADFAST LIFE

by

KRISTIN SCHMUCKER

Study Suggestions

Thank you for choosing this study to help you dig into God's Word. We are so passionate about women getting into Scripture, and we are praying that this study will be a tool to help you do that. Here are a few tips to help you get the most from this study:

––––––––

- Before you begin, take time to look into the context of the book. Find out who wrote it and learn about the cultural climate it was written in, as well as where it fits on the biblical timeline. Then take time to read through the entire book of the Bible we are studying if you are able. This will help you to get the big picture of the book and will aid in comprehension, interpretation, and application.

- Start your study time with prayer. Ask God to help you understand what you are reading and allow it to transform you (Psalm 119:18).

- Look into the context of the book as well as the specific passage.

- Before reading what is written in the study, read the assigned passage! Repetitive reading is one of the best ways to study God's Word. Read it several times, if you are able, before going on to the study. Read in several translations if you find it helpful.

- As you read the text, mark down observations and questions. Write down things that stand out to you, things that you notice, or things that you don't understand. Look up important words in a dictionary or interlinear Bible.

- Look for things like verbs, commands, and references to God. Notice key terms and themes throughout the passage.

- After you have worked through the text, read what is written in the study. Take time to look up any cross-references mentioned as you study.

- Then work through the questions provided in the book. Read and answer them prayerfully.

- Paraphrase or summarize the passage, or even just one verse from the passage. Putting it into your own words helps you to slow down and think through every word.

- Focus your heart on the character of God that you have seen in this passage. What do you learn about God from the passage you have studied? Adore Him and praise Him for who He is.

- Think and pray through application and how this passage should change you. Get specific with yourself. Resist the urge to apply the passage to others. Do you have sin to confess? How should this passage impact your attitude toward people or circumstances? Does the passage command you to do something? Do you need to trust Him for something in your life? How does the truth of the gospel impact your everyday life?

- We recommend you have a Bible, pen, highlighters, and journal as you work through this study. We recommend that ballpoint pens instead of gel pens be used in the study book to prevent smearing.

Here are several other optional resources that you may find helpful as you study:

———

- www.blueletterbible.org This free website is a great resource for digging deeper. You can find translation comparison, an interlinear option to look at words in the original languages, Bible dictionaries, and even commentary.

- A Dictionary. If looking up words in the Hebrew and Greek feels intimidating, look up words in English. Often times we assume we know the meaning of a word, but looking it up and seeing its definition can help us understand a passage better.

- A double-spaced copy of the text. You can use a website like www.biblegateway.com to copy the text of a passage and print out a double-spaced copy to be able to mark on easily. Circle, underline, highlight, draw arrows, and mark in any way you would like to help you dig deeper and work through a passage.

—

Now if any of you lacks wisdom, he should ask God—who gives to all generously and ungrudgingly—and it will be given to him. But let him ask in faith without doubting. For the doubter is like the surging sea, driven and tossed by the wind. That person should not expect to receive anything from the Lord, being double-minded and unstable in all his ways. Let the brother of humble circumstances boast in his exaltation.

TABLE OF CONTENTS

.DAY 1.

The Book
of James

James 1-5

The book of James contains five short chapters that are packed with practical theology. Due to its practical nature, it is a favorite among many believers. It calls us to a living faith and a steadfast life as we learn to live out the grace that has been shown to us by Jesus.

The authorship of the book of James is traditionally attributed to James who was the half-brother of Jesus. Though James was a skeptic during the ministry of Jesus, he is a changed man after the resurrection and would rise as a prominent church leader in the church in Jerusalem. James was martyred in AD 62 for his faith in Jesus, so we can be sure that the book was written before then. Most scholars date the book between AD 44-49 because it is believed that the letter was written before the Jerusalem council that took place in AD 49. This would have made it the first New Testament book to be written down, even before the Gospels would have been written.

James is writing to an audience of Christians. The first verse references the twelve tribes of the dispersion which has been interpreted in different ways. Some take this to mean that James is specifically writing to Jewish Christians. Others interpret this verse in a similar way as 1 Peter 1:1 where the term dispersion is used as a reference to the fact that Christians are strangers and exiles in this world. Because we as Christians have been adopted into the chosen people of God, the book has direct impact for us as the church of Jesus Christ as we seek to live out our faith.

The book of James falls within the category of the letters or epistles in the New Testament, but it also has a strong sense of wisdom literature. In many ways reading James reminds us of the Proverbs of the Old Testament. Where the Proverbs taught about how to live out the law, James teaches us how to live out our faith and have a life that is gospel-focused. James writes with the heart of a pastor as he seeks to guide and admonish his readers. In fact, the book contains about 59 commands or calls to obedience. James wants believers to obey and follow the Lord. The book of James is filled with many references to the Old Testament, and it contains an abundance of references to the teachings of Jesus, specifically to The Sermon on the Mount. It appears that James had gleaned much from the teachings of his half-brother, and the book of James calls us to live out the message of the upside-down kingdom that Jesus had proclaimed on earth.

The themes of James are numerous. The overarching themes are the practical life of a disciple of Jesus, and the relationship between faith and works. James digs even deeper into these topics by addressing things like: trials, obedience, our words, partiality, worldliness, wealth, suffering, and prayer. James is going to teach us about works and how we should live, but he does this in light of the gospel of God's grace. We are being taught in this short book how we should live because of God's grace in our lives. We are compelled to live a steadfast life.

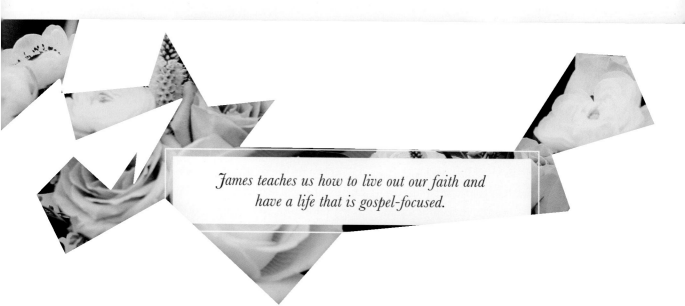

James teaches us how to live out our faith and have a life that is gospel-focused.

1. *Read through the entire book of James and write down the key themes you notice as you read.*

2. *What stood out to you the most as you read through the book of James?*

3. *Take time to write out a prayer asking God to help you in this study of the book of James.*

.DAY 2.

·················

*Servant
of Jesus*

James 1:1

As we open the book of James, we come to the introduction given by James in verse 1. From the start we see that James introduces himself as a servant of God and of the Lord Jesus Christ. James could introduce himself as the brother of Jesus to make the reader think highly of the author. Or he could mention his role as a leader in the Jerusalem church. But James does neither of these. He does not try to impress the audience with his own greatness, but instead calls himself a servant. The Greek here is *doulos*, which literally means "slave." This term for slave also gives us a deep sense of devotion to a person. For James that is Jesus Christ Himself. Jesus may be the brother of James, but James recognized Him as the Lord of all.

James is an especially interesting person in Scripture. As the half-brother of Jesus, he would have had close personal interaction with Jesus, and yet Scripture shows us that he did not always believe. Throughout the Gospels we see references to the fact that the family of Jesus did not believe (Mark 3:20-21, Mark 6:1-6, John 7:1-5). Perhaps it was jealousy of their brother or perhaps they were just too close to see at first that the one who had grown up in their home was the Son of God. But somewhere along the way everything changed for James. 1 Corinthians 15:1-7 tells us about how Jesus appeared to James after He resurrected, and we see Mary and the brothers of Jesus with the disciples after the ascension in Acts 1:14. James had doubted and pushed back against the ministry of his half-brother, but somewhere along the way, James had been captured by the grace of God. James would go on to be a leader in the church of Jerusalem and we see his ministry throughout the book of Acts. The grace of Jesus had transformed the heart of James and now James would write to the followers of Jesus to compel them to live in light of that amazing grace.

In this introductory verse, James not only identifies himself as a servant of God, but he also makes some big statements about the identity of Jesus. He identified Him with the title Lord. This is the Greek *Kyrios* and it is the Greek equivalent to the Hebrew *Adonai*. James was identifying Jesus as God by using this term for Him. No doubt is left in our mind that James had come to know that his half-brother was God in the flesh. James had come to know the miracle of the incarnation. Although God taking the form of flesh and dwelling among us (John 1:14) is something that we are well acquainted with, this truth should leave us in awe of the love God has for His people to save them. Christ is the other word that is used to describe Jesus, the Greek word is *Christos*. We are very familiar with this word, but may often forget to dwell on its meaning. This word identifies Jesus as the Messiah or the Anointed One. Jesus is the One who the people of God and all of the world had been waiting for. He is the One who had come to rescue and redeem. These descriptions of James for his brother remind us of the majesty of Jesus, and they remind us that we also are servants of God.

The letter is written to the twelve tribes that are dispersed. This language would be very familiar to the Jewish community as it spoke of the Old Testament exile and the twelve tribes of Israel. But this message is for the church as well who has been adopted into the family of Abraham (Galatians 3:7, 28-29, Romans 4:16, Galatians 6:16). James is writing to the people of God dispersed throughout the world just as 1 Peter would do. The words of the book of James ring out today just as they did in the first century. The book is overflowing with the truth of how we should live as servants of the Lord Jesus Christ.

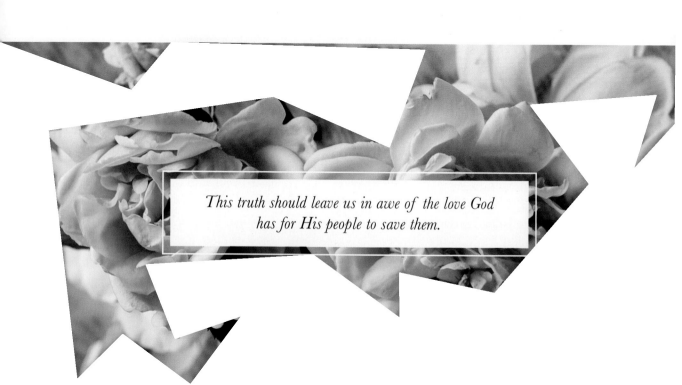

This truth should leave us in awe of the love God has for His people to save them.

1. *James identifies himself as a servant (or slave) of God. Read Romans 6:17-18. How does this further your understanding of what it means to be a slave of God?*

2. *In James 1:1, James describes who Jesus is for the reader. Take a moment below to describe Jesus in your own words.*

3. *Read Galatians 3:7, 28-29, Romans 4:16, and Galatians 6:16. How do these verses help your understanding of how believers have been made heirs of Abraham?*

. D A Y 3 .

Consider
it Joy

James 1:2-4

Consider your trials as joy. Our temptation when we read these verses may be to wonder if it is a misprint. We might be tempted to wonder why James is beginning his letter with this message. Why would James start this practical letter about the Christian life with a call to consider our trials as joy? James is speaking of the upside-down kingdom, just like Jesus did in the Sermon on the Mount. James knows that trials and suffering is a reality for all believers, and yet God can use even our suffering to draw our hearts to Him.

Counting our trials as joy doesn't really make sense to us, but that is what we are commanded to do. This is active and not passive. And it will not happen if we do not intentionally do it. This isn't going to happen when we are focused only on ourselves, but when we look to Christ and trust Him through the storms, we can see that His hand is in control of every moment of uncertainty. This is what James is telling us here. Nothing is left out. Trials come in so many ways, but because of Jesus we can count every one of them as joy. James uses a broad brush to tell us that every single one of our trials can be considered joy. Considering our trials as joy does not mean that we are happy about suffering; it means that we know that He will bring joy through them. Joy is not in spite of our suffering, but through our suffering.

Trials test us, but they do not test God. We are surprised by trials, but He never is. Trials serve to refine and prove our faith in God. The Greek here is not speaking of proof that a person has faith, but instead that it proves and tests, or refines and strengthens the already present faith of a believer just as gold is tested to strengthen and refine it. When we look at our trials, we do not need to ask, "Why me?" We can instead look at circumstances of our life and ask what we can learn from them. We can ask what God is teaching us and how God is growing us right where we are. We can count every trial as joy with full confidence that God will use every circumstance of our lives for our good and His glory. We can look to Jesus. We can follow the example He has given us (Hebrews 12:2), and trust that our trials are momentary, and there is joy that is set before us even in this.

We must preach truth to ourselves. Our minds must be grounded in the truth so that we can view our life from an eternal perspective. This perspective will guard us from our tendency to feel defeated in the midst of trials. We can trust that God is working even in the midst of our trials. He is working to build our endurance or steadfastness which will result in our spiritual maturity. As we set our hearts on knowing the Lord, we can find joy even in our trials because we know that they are growing us to be more like Him.

God is sovereign over our suffering. We can trust His sovereign hand to be faithful every step of the way. The trials that we face produce steadfastness or endurance and the result is that we are mature and complete, lacking absolutely nothing. We cannot be what God has called us to be without suffering. God uses our trials to bring us to maturity. The road of sanctification is paved with stones of suffering.

Our minds must be grounded in the truth so that we can view our life from an eternal perspective.

1 *What things in your life can you look back from and see either how God has brought good from them, or how God has grown you through them?*

2 *Why is it important that we remember that trials do not surprise God?*
How does that give you hope?

3 *Read Hebrews 12:2-3. How does the suffering of Jesus encourage you in your own trials and suffering? In James we are told to consider our trials as joy, but what are we told to consider in Hebrews 12:3? What is the result listed at the end of verse 3?*

. D A Y 4 .

Ask in
Faith

If we ask
for wisdom
He will give it

James 1:5-8

We do not need to ask for our trials to go away, but instead we should ask for the wisdom to trust God in them. James moves from teaching us about how trials grow and mature us and how we can count our trials as joy to instructing us to ask God for wisdom. This is the wisdom that only He can give. James ended verse four by telling us that as we mature, we will lack nothing. Then he ironically tells us that if we lack wisdom, we can ask God for it. This promise is sure. It is a prayer that we can pray and know that He will answer with a yes. If we ask for wisdom, He will give it.

What is wisdom? Wisdom is discernment and insight. It is the application of knowledge. In a biblical context it is the ability to discern the truth and walk in the wisdom of God. In fact, in 1 Corinthians 1:24-25 we see that Jesus is the wisdom of God. We cannot know true wisdom apart from Him. God's wisdom stands in stark contrast to the wisdom of the world. And the world will look at the wisdom of God and think that it is foolishness, but it is actually the way of the world that is foolish in the sight of God. This is the message of the upside-down kingdom that Jesus spoke of in The Sermon on The Mount in Matthew 5-7. In the kingdom of God, the last are first. In the kingdom of God those who mourn their sin are comforted, the persecuted and poor in spirit inherit the kingdom, and those who hunger for righteousness are satisfied. It is the wisdom of God and the truth of the upside-down kingdom that allows us to have joy in trials and to trust God when things don't make sense.

He calls us to ask in faith. We must have faith to trust God when we find ourselves in the upside-down kingdom and faith to trust His plan when suffering comes our way. The wisdom of God is trusting Him in every season. Double-minded here is the opposite of faith. It is the opposite of wisdom. We are double-minded when we pray, but also try to do things our own way. We are double-minded when we say that we surrender, and then we are overcome with the anxiety and worry of our situation. We are double-minded when we say that we are laying our burdens before Him, and then we pick them back up again. When we find ourselves giving into being double-minded, the remedy is repentance. We repent and then we ask Him to give us His wisdom. He is the Giver and He has an infinite supply of grace and wisdom for His people.

In Mark 9:14-29, a father comes to Jesus asking for healing for his son. He knows that Jesus can do it but is weary of all the years of struggle. In verse 23 he speaks to Jesus and says, "I believe, help my unbelief." This man knew that Jesus was the answer, but he still struggled to understand and trust. This passage is not telling us that we will never struggle. Rather, it is telling us that we must trust Him through the struggle. The father in Mark 9 was not double-minded. He was transparent before God and Jesus would heal his son that day. Faith doesn't mean that we never struggle, but it means that we know where to take those struggles.

We must ask God for the wisdom to view our life and trials in light of the truth. We need to have our minds renewed so that we can understand God's plan through testing (Romans 12:2-3). We need His wisdom so that we can understand our life in light of verses 2-4. We need His wisdom to know that we will not always understand, but we can always trust. We need our minds to be rooted in the truth of His Word so that we will be able to live in wisdom.

The wisdom of God is trusting Him in every season.

(1) *What situations in your life right now do you need wisdom in?*

(2) *Where do people often run for wisdom? Where should we run for wisdom?*

(3) *Look up the words "wisdom" and "unstable" and write the definitions below. What are the differences between the two?*

. DAY 5 .

Blessed is
the one who
loved Him

James 1:9-12

We are quick to compare. We are quick to think that someone else has a better situation than we do. We scroll social media and wonder why it seems that others have a better _____ (fill in the blank) than we do. James uses the contrast of wealth and poverty to illustrate spiritual truth for us. James uses an illustration that many of us can understand, but we can also think about other situations in our life in which we are tempted to compare. From singleness and marriage to motherhood and infertility, to the struggles we face in comparing our marriages, our weight, and even our gifts and talents, we are prone to compare ourselves to each other. James seeks to point our attention to the things that are eternal and ultimately to point our attention to the Eternal One.

In the context of the various trials that we face in this life, we may be tempted to think that when it comes to poverty and wealth, poverty is the trial. But that is not the case that James will make for us. Whether we find ourselves with great financial resources or we find ourselves with little, our temptation is to seek satisfaction in the things of this world instead of in Jesus. For the person who has little, this may be evidenced in a pursuit of more or a lack of trust in God to supply what we need. For the person with wealth, the temptation may be to think that they have earned it all themselves or to devote their time to the accumulation of wealth. Whether rich or poor we are in danger of living a life in pursuit of the things of this world. But James is telling us that there is a greater thing to pursue. There is a greater One to pursue.

The instructions of James to the lowly and the rich are the same though they may appear different. To the lowly, he tells them to recognize that wealth does not change a person's status with God. We are valuable to God because we are His people, not because of what we have. To the wealthy, he encourages them to remember that no matter how much they have, he is poor without the love of Christ. Even with vast financial resources, we are poor beggars apart from Jesus. The things of this world will never satisfy, but Jesus satisfies the soul. Earthly wealth or the lack of it is temporary, but God is eternal, and His Word is eternal. We may hear some familiar words from Isaiah 40:7-8 as James contrasts the things that do not last, with the Word of God that stands forever. The eternal is greater than the temporal. Our eyes are easily distracted by this world's flashing lights, but the glory of God shines far brighter than the glitter of this world.

Blessed. It is the first word of the Sermon on the Mount and James begins verse twelve with it as well. And just as Jesus did in the sermon, James references the upside-down kingdom. He tells us that blessing comes to those that endure trials. It is backwards and upside-down, but that is how the kingdom of God works. The crown of life is promised to those that endure. For James' original readers, the word crown would not have brought to mind the crown of royalty, but instead the wreath placed on the head of an athlete at the end of a race. This is the reward for faithfulness and endurance. There is reward for walking through the trials of this life in faithfulness. Jesus is standing at the finish line cheering us on, but He is also with us. He not only runs with us, but carries us through this race. We run the race in union and communion with Him. The blessing here is blessing that only God can give. It is the blessing reserved for those who love Him. This world tries to pull our gaze to the temporary, but we shift our gaze to the Eternal One. He is altogether lovely. He is worthy of worship and worthy of all of our hearts. The life of blessing is reserved for those who love Him.

The things of this world will never satisfy, but Jesus satisfies the soul.

1) *In what areas are you tempted to compare in?*

2) *How can both poverty and wealth distract from God?*

3) *Read Matthew 5:2-12. How does James 1:12 echo these words of Jesus in The Sermon on The Mount? Write below what Jesus and James say that a blessed life looks like.*

"
*the testing
of your faith
produces
endurance*
"

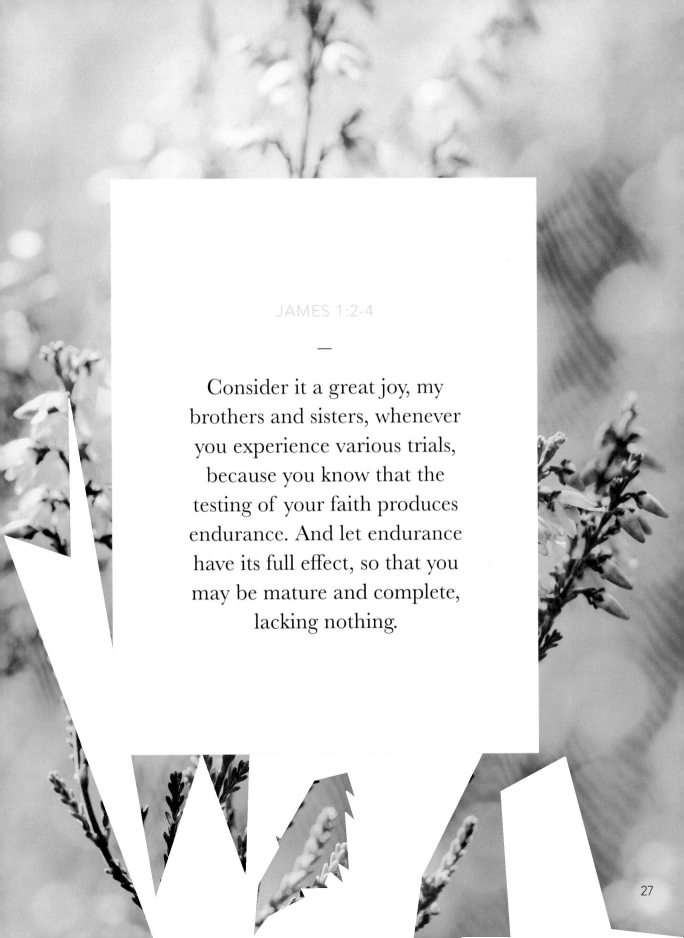

JAMES 1:2-4

—

Consider it a great joy, my
brothers and sisters, whenever
you experience various trials,
because you know that the
testing of your faith produces
endurance. And let endurance
have its full effect, so that you
may be mature and complete,
lacking nothing.

Weekly Reflection JAMES 1:1-12

Paraphrase the passage from this week.

What did you observe from this week's text about God and His character?

What does the passage teach about the condition of mankind and about yourself?

How does this passage point to the gospel?

_____

_____

_____

_____

_____

_____

_____

_____

How should you respond to this passage? What is the personal application?

What specific action steps can you take this week to apply the passage?

_____

_____

_____

_____

_____

_____

· DAY 1 ·

· · · · · · · · · · · · · · ·

Trials and
Temptations

James 1:13-15

James has been teaching us about God's sovereign purpose in our trials and how God uses trials to grow and mature us. Now he pauses for a moment to remind us of the important truth that though God tests us, He is never the One who tempts us.

It would be easy for us to look at our trials and to think that God was unjust in giving them to us, or to even wonder if God was setting us up to sin by putting difficulty in our path. James proactively addresses the question that he knows will arise. He reminds us that we are sinful, but God is sinless. He cannot be tempted, and He does not tempt us. James is showing us that there are two very different ways that we can react to trials. We can allow God to use them to refine and mature us, or we can allow them to cause bitterness in our hearts toward God as we choose to spiral into sin.

The blaming of God for our sin is not something new. In fact, the Old Testament is full of times when God's people blame Him. Even in Genesis 3 we find Adam shifting blame. Though at first glance it seems he is blaming Eve, he is really blaming God who is the one who gave Him Eve. Eve quickly blames the serpent for her sin as well. We are not so different from our first parents. Our first instinct is consistently to find somewhere to shift the blame. If we can't shift it to a person, we look for a circumstance or situation. And ultimately the root of all of these accusations is an accusation against God Himself.

Adam and Eve may have been the first humans to shift blame, but they certainly would not be the last. In Exodus 15 the people sing the Song of Moses as they rejoice in God's favor and how He had delivered them out of slavery in Egypt. God had triumphantly brought them through the Red Sea on dry land and had destroyed their enemies before their eyes. The people are overwhelmed with gratitude and praise for God's goodness to them, but by the end of the chapter things have changed. The people have no water and they begin to complain. Though God had parted a great sea, they did not trust Him to give them water to drink. The incident wasn't isolated and through the rest of the book of Exodus, the people would grumble and complain and fail to see that God was teaching them to trust Him. The examples stretch past Genesis and Exodus and in fact the whole Old Testament is a record of God's covenant faithfulness to His people and their unfaithfulness to Him. Their perspective was wrong. God was consistently gracious and faithful, but the sin in their own hearts caused them to sin and brought great consequences.

James shows us the spiral of sin. We are tempted, enticed, and lured away by our own desires, and those desires lead us to disobedience, and that sin and disobedience to God brings about death. We are tempted not by God, but by our own sinful desires. We are allured by sin. We are lured or drawn away by it. The word in the Greek gives the idea of a hunter luring his prey. But sadly, James tells us that we are doing this to ourselves. We convince ourselves we can dabble in sin. Then we convince ourselves that we won't go too far. Then we try to convince ourselves that our sin is not that bad, but the consequences soon follow. And where there is sin, there is always death.

God sets before us two paths. Trials and suffering are sure in this life, but we have a choice in how we respond to them. We can choose to count all of our trials as joy and grow and mature, or we can allow our trials to lead us down the dangerous and deathly path of sin. James exhorts us to choose life. Though the path of sin brings death, he has already told us that the path of endurance through trials leads us to the crown of life. He pleads with us to choose life.

Trials and suffering are sure in this life, but we have a choice in how we respond to them.

1   *In what ways are we tempted to blame others or God for our sin?*

2   *Read Exodus 15. At the beginning of the chapter the people's eyes are on God and they are worshiping Him. But by chapter 22 they turn their eyes to their circumstances and they begin to complain. How does keeping our eyes on God allow us to have a correct perspective? How do we keep our eyes on Him?*

3   *What is the difference between testing and temptation?*

.DAY 2.

....

Every good and perfect gift is from Him

James 1:16-17

Immediately after warning us about trials and temptations comes the command to not be deceived. This command is only necessary if there is a reason for it, and there is great reason for this warning. It is needed because the world will try to deceive us. It is needed because the enemy will try to deceive us. It is needed because we will try to deceive ourselves. James punctuates this command with the term beloved and in this he shows us his urgency in this command. James speaks to those who are beloved in the body of Christ, but he also speaks to believers who are beloved by Jesus Himself. James knows that we will be tempted to be deceived and he warns us to be watchful.

In verse 17 he continues by telling us that we will be tempted to believe that there are good things that are being withheld from us. The temptation is to believe that God is holding out on us. And this temptation is as old as the garden of Eden (Genesis 3). The crafty serpent sought to convince Eve that God was withholding something from her by forbidding her to eat of the tree. Our temptations are often the same. We are tempted to believe that there is some satisfaction in the sin that God has forbidden, or that we will find happiness somewhere other than God's perfect will. God has given us everything that we need to serve Him, and if He has withheld something from us it is because He knows it is not good for us right now. God is holding nothing good back from His people.

We must preach this truth to our hearts that Jesus is all we need. And if Jesus is all we need, we don't need a dream house to be happy. If Jesus is all we need, we don't need the approval of others to feel worthy. If Jesus is all we need, we don't need to lose ten pounds or get a new wardrobe to be content. If Jesus is all we need, we don't need our days to go smoothly because true peace and contentment are found in Him alone. If Jesus is really all we need, our joy is not dependent on our circumstances but on Him. And that means that we can find joy and peace in Him right in the midst of the chaos, the stressful, and the mundane. We can trust that He has given us what is good for us and that where He has us is where He wants us. The knowledge that all He does is good frees us to trust Him even when our lives do not make sense or look the way that we thought that they would.

All that is good for us and everything that we have comes from our Father. James uses the phrase Father of lights in these verses. Throughout the Scriptures God is described as light and the creator of light. In a culture that often included the worship of light and the celestial beings, these words declare that our God is the only one who should be worshiped and that He is the one who created the sun, moon, and stars. Not only did God create the celestial beings, but He is also distinct from them. They change, move, and create shadows, but He is unchanging and steadfast. We never have to worry about Him changing. He does not change, and yet He holds the power to change us. He transforms our darkness into light. Just as He called forth the light from the darkness in Genesis 1, He has shone in our hearts (2 Corinthians 4:6).

We do not need to be deceived by the lies of the enemy, the lies of the world, or even the lies that we tell ourselves. We can be confident in the Word and character of God and know that every good and perfect gift has been given to us through God. He gave us the most perfect gift at the cross through the sacrifice of Jesus and it is through Christ and in Christ that we find every spiritual blessing (Ephesians 1:3). We can rest secure in a God who has freely given us His Son and will give us all things that are good for us (Romans 8:32). Jesus is all that we need.

All that is good for us and everything that we have comes from our Father.

1. *Why do you think that James commands us not to be deceived?*

2. *How are we deceived? Of the three things that try to deceive us, which one have you experienced most?*

3. *How do these verses comfort you?*

. DAY 3 .

By the
Word of
Truth

James 1:18

Every good perfect gift comes from the Father. And the greatest gift that He has ever given is His Son. Jesus is the greatest gift. Verse 18 is small, yet it is packed with the message of the gospel. It begins with the truth that our salvation is not our own doing, but it is by the choosing of our God. Without God there is no good in us and no desire for what is right. Yet when we we're running far from God, He chose us. God in His free will has chosen us to be His people. He set His love on us and pursued us. In His initiating love He caused us to be born again (1 Peter 1:3). Though we could not in ourselves choose Him, He has chosen us (John 15:16). When we were far from God, the Father in His grace and mercy has drawn us to Himself (John 6:44). When we were hopeless, He gave us a sure hope.

The words of James that God has brought us forth bring to mind the words of Jesus to Nicodemus that we must be born again (John 3:1-21). We have no power on our own, no righteousness of our own, yet God in His love has brought us forth and given us new birth and new life. There was nothing we could do to earn His love, yet He loved us. While we were still sinners and enemies of God, Christ died for us (Romans 5:6-11). And we can be confident that since there was nothing that we could do to earn His free gift of salvation, there is nothing that we can do to lose it. Our salvation has been given and secure by the gracious love of the Father.

Salvation and new life are given to us by the word of truth. These words appear at other parts of the New Testament such as 1 Peter 1:23-25 where we are told that we have been born again through the living and abiding word of God. 1 Peter 1:25 clearly interprets this for us when it tells us that this word is the good news or the gospel. In Ephesians 1:13 we see that the word of truth is the gospel of our salvation. The Word of God shines forth the message of the gospel. And the gospel is the conduit through which God has chosen to save His people. The gospel is the message of Jesus. It is the message of the cross.

We have been chosen by Him and we have been born again through the power of the gospel, and now we see that we are a kind of firstfruits. The concept of the firstfruit offering may not be one that we are familiar with. Firstfruits is described throughout the Old Testament (Deuteronomy 26, Leviticus 23:10-14). The first product of the harvest would be set apart and offered to the Lord. It was a declaration of the faithfulness of God and a reminder of the covenant. Through it the people of Israel proclaimed that God keeps His promises. In this same way the New Testament draws on the Old Testament and declares that we are the firstfruits of His creatures. Those who have

been redeemed declare the faithfulness of God. We are set apart for Him and are a declaration of His covenant faithfulness to redeem a people for Himself. Jesus is also referred to as the firstfruits and our status is secured because of our union with Him (1 Corinthians 15:20-23). Romans 8:18-23 tells us that we are the firstfruits of the restoration of the world. All of creation groans, but we as the firstfruits in the Spirit are the declaration of God's faithfulness. Just as God has brought new life to us, He will bring a new heaven and a new earth. He will be faithful to every word of His promise.

He has chosen us in His initiating love. He has saved us and displayed His faithfulness to us by the power of the gospel. Our response to these beautiful truths can only be to trust Him, to love Him, and to obey Him. For the gift of the gospel, we pour out an offering of praise to the Giver of all good things.

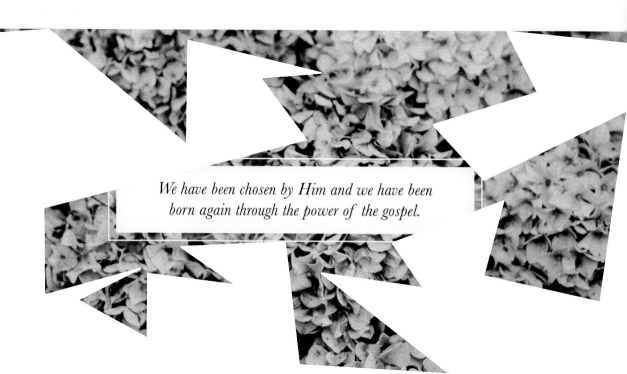

We have been chosen by Him and we have been born again through the power of the gospel.

1. *Paraphrase James 1:18.*

2. *Read John 3:1-21. What does it mean to be born again?*

3. *How do believers display the faithfulness of God?*

. DAY 4 .

. . . .

Receive the implanted Word

be quick to hear
slow to speak
slow to anger

James 1:19-21

James is beginning to shift our focus. Up until this point we have been focused on how we should respond to trials and temptations, and now James shifts the focus to how we should respond to the word of truth implanted in us. How should a believer live and respond to the Word of God? James begins by addressing the beloved brothers and sisters again. He wants them to know and be assured of the truth that he is about to speak to them. He wants this knowledge to go past just their minds and be settled in their hearts.

He commands the believers here to be quick to hear, slow to speak, and slow to anger. These verses are typically taken in the context of our human relationships and they definitely have an application there. But in context (see verse 19 as well as verses 22, 23, and 25), it seems that James may also be pointing us to the way that we should respond not only in our human relationships, but also to the truth of the Word of God. As we come to God's Word, we should be quick to listen to what God is speaking through the Scriptures. We should be slow to speak and slow to become angry. Speaking and anger prevent us from hearing, so we are commanded to stop and listen to the Word. We should not come to the Word with our own presupposed ideas or be angry when we are convicted of sin. Instead we should come humbly with a heart ready to hear from the Word of God.

These principles hold great wisdom for our relationships as well. They should govern our most important relationship with our Savior as well as the relationships with those who He has so graciously placed in our lives. We display godly character as we practice in all relationships being quick to hear, slow to speak, and slow to anger.

The Word of God that gave us new birth now shows us how to live a new life. James uses the picture of salvation to show how we should come to Scriptures again and again. Salvation happens only once, and yet we are also constantly growing in sanctification and into salvation. Our salvation is a past tense event that has future implications, and that we are daily growing in. James is telling us that in the same way that we received the gift of salvation, we grow in sanctification. Our salvation is given to us by God through the Word of the gospel, and we continue to grow through the Word of the gospel. The gospel is not just for the moment of salvation. The gospel is for every day. The gospel is what we must preach to ourselves daily.

We are commanded to put away our sin and all filthiness and wickedness. Then as we hear the Word (v 19), we receive it. We are commanded to receive it with meekness or humility. This humility flows out of hearts fully convinced of the truth of the gospel that there is nothing that we could do to earn God's love and yet He loved us anyway. As we see and know the character of God through His Word our hearts are humbled before

Him. This humility is the opposite of our fleshly tendencies that were found in verses 19-20 to be more prone to speak and be angry than to listen and be humble.

James speaks of the Word as the implanted word. In his phrasing, he references the great new covenant passages of the prophets and the declaration that God would give new hearts and write the word on our hearts (Jeremiah 31:31-33, Ezekiel 36:24-27). As believers who have been transformed by the gospel, we have been given new hearts. Daily we battle against our still present sinful flesh and the new heart that we have been given. James is telling us to continue on in pursuit of the Lord. He encourages us to come to the Word just as we came to Christ, through hearing the Word, believing the Word, and responding to the Word.

What a gift it is to grow in the Word day by day. To observe the character of God and allow Him to transform us into His image. This is the life of sanctification. We are called to hear, believe, and respond.

The gospel is for every day.

1   *In relationship to God's Word, what does it look like to be quick to hear, slow to speak, and slow to anger?*

2   *In relationship to other people, what does it look like to be quick to hear, slow to speak, and slow to anger? Is there someone in your life that you need to specifically practice this with this week?*

3   *Read Jeremiah 31:31-33 and Ezekiel 36:24-27. How do these passages give insight into what it means to have the Word implanted in our hearts?*

. DAY 5 .

....

Doers of the Word

James 1:22-25

Be doers of the Word. This is the message of the James and verse 22 is the theme that echoes through this short book. The Bible calls us to do something about what we have read. The Bible calls us to become more like the author. This call to obedience and transformation is not in our own strength, but through the power of the gospel. In these short verses James tells us the theme of this entire book and gives us an example to imprint the truth on our hearts.

Genuine faith transforms us. We are called to not just be those who hear the Word of God, though it is essential that we hear it. We are called to be those who hear and those who obey. The words from James are strong. If we hear the Word and we do not obey it, we are deceiving ourselves. That is a strong indictment, but the words call to mind the words of Jesus in Matthew 7:21-27. Both Jesus and James are driving home a strong point that we must heed. There are those who claim to be followers of Jesus, and come to church, and look the part, but they are not believers. We deceive ourselves if we think that we can claim the name of Christ and even study our Bibles and not obey what He has told us to do. James is not telling us in any way that salvation comes from works. Scripture teaches us clearly that our salvation is by grace alone through faith alone and totally apart from our works (Ephesians 2:8-9). Instead, James is telling us that our works are an evidence of our salvation. Our outward fruit points toward an inward transformation.

James then gives us an illustration to help us understand. He tells us that those who only hear the Word are like those who look in the mirror and then walk away and forget what they look like. What use is it to look in the mirror and see a dirty face and messy hair and then walk away without washing our face and brushing our hair? In contrast, the one who hears and obeys is like a person that looks in the mirror and then changes based on what they see. The gospel demands obedience.

James refers to the perfect law which is the law of liberty. In context, we can see that he is referring to God's Word, but more specifically this perfect law of liberty is the gospel. We must view all of Scripture in light of the gospel, and our obedience must be rooted in the gospel. It is the gospel that enables us to obey. In our own strength and in our own power, we cannot obey or be doers of the Word. But because we have been transformed by the gospel and given new life as a new creation (2 Corinthians 5:17). We have been made new. We have been united with Christ. We are in Him. As believers, we can be doers of the Word because the God of the Word lives inside us. It is the power of the Word that enables us to be doers of

the Word. And obedience brings freedom. The life of obedience is not the life of legalism. Legalism gives only the appearance of spirituality while living apart from the gospel and in our own strength. But the obedience that we are called to is obedience that is rooted in the gospel just as the gospel is implanted in us.

But the good news of the gospel for our obedience is that though Jesus calls us to obey, He also gives us the power to do it. This power to obey is not from ourselves, but from Him. In Matthew 11:28-30 Jesus tells us to come and take His yoke upon us. The burden of living in our own strength is too heavy for us to bear, but there is rest in obedience. There is rest in humble surrender. There is rest in a heart submitted to the Lord. We find rest in obedience through the power of the gospel that reminds us that our obedience is only made possible because we are in Christ and He is in us.

We must view all of Scripture in light of the gospel, and our obedience must be rooted in the gospel.

1   *What does it look like practically to be a doer of the Word?*

2   *How does the gospel enable us to obey?*

3   *Rad Matthew 11:28-30. How can we find rest in obedience?*

"
**and it will be
given to him**
"

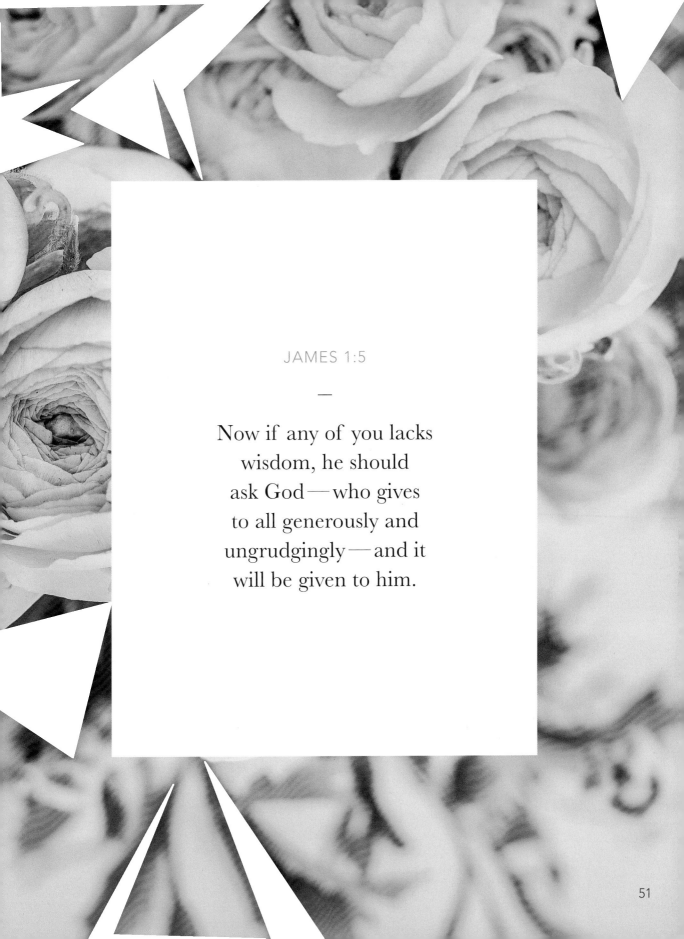

JAMES 1:5

—

Now if any of you lacks
wisdom, he should
ask God — who gives
to all generously and
ungrudgingly — and it
will be given to him.

Weekly Reflection JAMES 1:13-25

Paraphrase the passage from this week.

What did you observe from this week's text about God and His character?

What does the passage teach about the condition of mankind and about yourself?

How does this passage point to the gospel?

How should you respond to this passage? What is the personal application?

What specific action steps can you take this week to apply the passage?

.DAY 1.

·················

Pure Religion

the gospel transforms every aspect of our being

James 1:26-27

James has been telling us that we need to hear and receive the Word of God, and now he tells us that we also need to act on it. Faith works. Faith is active. The life of faith is not accepting Jesus and then living the same old way. Faith in the gospel changes everything. The Christian life is not just about giving our hearts to Jesus, but about surrendering every word, thought, deed, attitude and moment to Him. The gospel transforms every aspect of our being. It transforms our hearts to be more like God. The gospel calls us to a life of radical and ordinary obedience. In the big and in the small we surrender. In the monumental and the mundane we worship. We serve because we are in Christ and He is in us.

In these two short verses, James speaks of three life-changing principles. In fact, it is these three things that the entire rest of the book will be devoted to expounding upon. We are in no way saved by the works that we do, but as believers who have been transformed by the gospel, our faith is evidenced by the things that we do. The gospel makes us new creations. It speaks light into the darkness. The gospel changes our view of everything.

The first thing that James addresses is our words. He tells us that if we do not bridle our tongues our religion is worthless. His language is strong, and James has a lot to say in this short book about our words and the power of our tongue. Our words are key because they reveal what is going on in our hearts (Matthew 12:34). A problem with our words is really a problem with our hearts. Our words show who we truly are. James tells us that we must bridle, harness, or control our words. The warning

55

is strong that if we cannot control our words through the power of the Holy Spirit, we are deceiving ourselves about our spiritual condition. James is calling us to allow the gospel to transform our hearts and in turn transform our words.

The next thing that James tells us is that our care for the widow and the orphan is a mark of pure religion. The widow and orphan are those who are overlooked and marginalized. James is calling us to a sacrificial and selfless life. He is calling us to give to those who may never be able to give anything in return. Adoption is one way in which the body of Christ can reach out to the most vulnerable in our society. Perhaps God is stirring in your heart toward adoption, or perhaps you can be used to help someone else who feels called to adopt. Instead of using our voices for evil, we can raise our voices to speak for those who cannot speak for themselves. We can speak up for those who have been neglected and forgotten. We can be a friend to those who feel unwelcome and out of place.

This goes far beyond just the orphan and the widow and extends to just about every group of people. It could be refugees and immigrants who feel like they don't belong. It could be minorities, single moms, and singles who feel out of place in our churches. It could be a lonely friend who is struggling or a tired new mom. We image God when we reach out to those who need comfort and encouragement. In fact, the word here translated as visit or look after could also be translated as seek after and the New Testament is full of times when we see that God has sought or visited His people (Luke 1:68, Luke 7:17, Acts 15:14). We should love others the way that God has loved us.

The last admonition that James gives in these verses is for us to stay unstained from the world. This is instruction that can apply to every area of our life. We are to be holy and set apart to serve the Lord. We are commanded not to think or act like the world. And this call to holiness is one that will spread to every area of our lives. It impacts areas of purity and personal holiness as we do not do some of the things that the world does. It impacts how we treat others as we do not buy into the lie of the world that anyone that is different than us is bad. It impacts how we speak, act, think, and live. It calls us to be Christ-like in every part of who we are.

The call of the book of James is the call to be like Jesus. It is the call to be transformed by the power of the gospel and to live and love like Jesus.

1. *In what ways do you struggle with your words? What sin do your words reveal? Ask God to help you in this area.*

2. *What are some actionable ways that you can love and serve others to carry out the command of James 1:27?*

3. *In what areas have you seen the thinking of the world creep into your heart?*

.DAY 2.

Show no
Partiality

James 2:1-4

Without taking a break, James launches into his next section. In these verses he warns of the sin of partiality. It seems like an odd thing to begin with, and we could even be tempted to think that it is a trivial matter compared to what we may think are much greater sins and temptations for God's people. But James is convinced that this is important, and through the leading of the Holy Spirit, he commands us to abstain from showing partiality of any kind.

At its foundation partiality is contrary to and incompatible with the gospel. From the start of the Bible we learn that man and woman are made in the image of God (Genesis 1:27). So partiality is an attack of the *imago dei* that is etched into every human who has been made in God's image. When we partake in the sin of partiality to any extent, we show that we do not truly understand the gospel. The message of the gospel is that Jesus has broken down every barrier whether cultural, racial, economic, or religious. Jesus has proclaimed the message of salvation to all who will believe. In fact, 2 Corinthians 8:9 tells us that Jesus Himself became poor so that we could become rich. Jesus reached through social barriers and rescued the weak and the lowly, and as we read the gospel, we are shocked to find that those farthest from the kingdom of God are often the seemingly religious.

James' words are direct as he plainly commands us to show no partiality. Yet he also encourages us as those who hold to faith in Jesus. His words are encouragement to press on in this life and live in a way that is different and distinct from the world around us. In one of only two mentions of Jesus by name (the other is in James 1:1), James describes Jesus as the Lord Jesus Christ and the Lord of Glory or the glorious

Lord Jesus. James is affirming the truth that Jesus is the Christ or the Messiah. He is also setting Him before us as the Glorious One. We see the glory of God when we look to Jesus who is the embodiment of God's glory among us (John 1:14). And once glimpse of God's glory changes our perspective. A glimpse of the glory of God reminds us that even the richest of earth is a pauper before the sovereign Creator.

In verses 2-3 James gives us an example of partiality. The example may seem exaggerated or over the top, but it causes us to think deeply about our own tendencies to honor those who we deem important and worthy, and to neglect those who seem lesser. We crave attention from those who we think are important. We want their approval. And we even seek for others to know that they approve of us. We are quick to pour our time and energy into those who are deemed important, and we are quick to brush off those who seem like a burden to us. We are annoyed by people who God has made. These sins reveal a heart issue in us and we must repent. Jesus gave His life for the rich and the poor, the somebodies and the nobodies, and we should pour out our lives in service for every person made in His image.

James makes it clear that participation in this kind of partiality is not just unkind, but it is sinful. So what do we do when we sense that we have at certain times or even currently participated in partiality? We repent. We turn to the Lord and we ask Him to restore us. And He will. We turn from seeking the favor of people and we seek to please God alone. We remind ourselves that the wealthy of society and the most popular in our churches are just as valuable to God as the homeless on the corner and the spiritually struggling. We need a vision of humanity the way that God sees them. We need a heart that sees people as made in the image of God with souls that need the message of the gospel and the hope of Jesus. And the same gospel that can save the lost is the gospel that can continually transform our own hearts and make us more like Jesus.

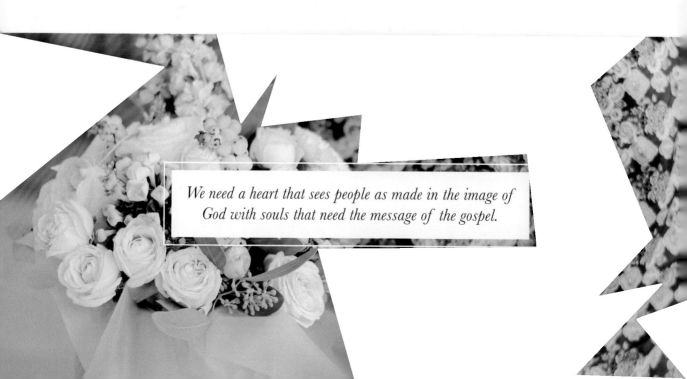

We need a heart that sees people as made in the image of God with souls that need the message of the gospel.

1. *In what ways have you seen partiality? What things tend to be respected? What tends to be looked down on?*

2. *Have you ever seen someone show partiality to one person over another? Have you ever felt this creep into your own heart?*

3. *How is partiality contrary and incompatible with the gospel?*

. DAY 3 .

Heirs of the Kingdom

James 2:5-7

Listen up. James continues speaking on the topic of the favoritism that was prevalent with a call for his readers who are his beloved brothers and sisters to listen up to the words that he is speaking. It seems that James' illustration in verses 2-3 was a hypothetical one, but now he is shifting the tone a bit and getting personal. He is about to speak directly to those who are guilty of this exact thing. James is showing us that this is about a posture of our hearts. You don't need to be rich to dishonor the poor and show favoritism. In fact, James is likely speaking to an audience that is predominantly poor as was the case for most of the early church. He wants them to see past the surface and understand that this is an issue of their hearts.

James calls our minds back to the fact that God in His sovereignty had chosen the poor of the world to be children of God. He is not stating that God had only chosen the poor, but that He had also chosen the poor. God has called His people from every tribe, tongue, and nation. He calls them from the rich and the poor, the wealthy and the lowly. And yet at the same time all throughout Scripture we can see that God has a special care and concern for the poor, the weak, the helpless, and the marginalized. Scripture overflows with God's personal care for the poor and also His commands for His people to care for the poor (Deuteronomy 10:17-19). If we show favoritism, we are denying the truth of the gospel message and standing in contrast to the character of God.

Jesus Himself came as a poor man. He was not born in a palace, but was laid in a manger. And through the entire ministry of Jesus, it was the religious who scorned Him for His interaction with the poor, the sinners, and the social outcasts.

2 Corinthians 8:9 reminds us that Jesus became poor and took on the humble form of a human so that we might become rich. It is interesting to note that this verse is found in the context of a call to generosity. Because when we recognize the generosity that God has shown us, it should overflow in generosity to others. When we see that God has chosen us when we were spiritually poor, it compels us to show the love and grace of God to every person that we meet whether rich or poor.

The wording of verse 5 though speaking of literal poverty is also a clear allusion to the words of Jesus in the Sermon on the Mount when He said, "Blessed are the poor in Spirit, for theirs is the kingdom of God." The tangible poverty of the world points us to the far greater reality of our spiritual poverty. Whether our bank accounts are full or empty, we are all spiritually poor before God. We are brought low by our need before Him, and then He fills our cup to overflowing with His grace. It is the spiritually poor who inherit the kingdom. We should have compassion on the ma-

terial poverty of others because we know what it is like to be spiritually bankrupt.

In James' day, the poor were the weak, the vulnerable, and the despised. This is often true today as well, but in order for us to fully live out what James is commending us to do, we must care for all people who our society rejects. We stay unstained from the world when we reject the world's way of thinking and do not participate in any sort of favoritism inside or outside the doors of the church building (James 1:27). The believer should extend open arms to the poor, the socially awkward, the marginalized, children, the disabled, the elderly, the refugee, the immigrant, and the rejected. The call of Jesus is for all to come, and if the church rejects those who seem too far or too sinful or too different, we are not practicing "true religion." As followers of Jesus we carry His name with us in our title of Christian. James exhorts us to represent our Savior well to the world around us.

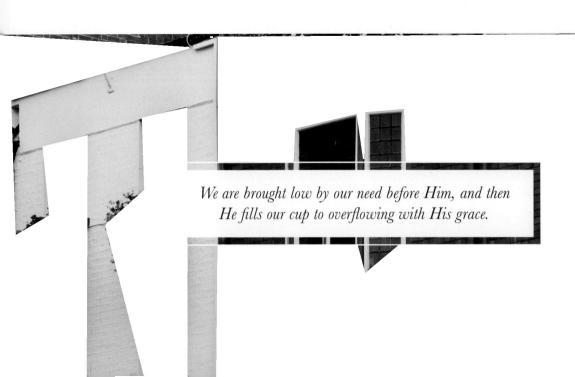

*We are brought low by our need before Him, and then
He fills our cup to overflowing with His grace.*

1. *Read Deuteronomy 10:17-19. How does this passage present God's heart for the marginalized and the heart that we should have for them as well?*

2. *Can you think of any groups of people who are often not accepted by Christians?*

3. *How should our understanding of our spiritual poverty apart from Christ change the way we view the poor of this world?*

. DAY 4 .

....

Mercy Triumphs

we have no power
in us apart
from Christ

James 2:8-13

At the end of chapter one, James told us about the things that were evidences of pure religion, and sadly in our own strength we fail every test. But the good news is that our weakness to fulfill these tests of pure religion points us to our need for the glorious gospel that blots out our transgressions and compels us to walk in holiness.

James speaks of the royal law and tells us that it is good if we fulfill it. This royal law is according to Scripture. It is the law of God. The law of the Kingdom. It is the law of King Jesus. Jesus spoke in Matthew 18:21-35 of the two commandments that sum up all the law and the prophets. If we could just love the Lord our God above all else, and love our neighbors as we love ourselves, we would be good to go on the path of following this law. The problem is we can't do it. We have no power in us apart from Christ to obey these commands that were first given back in Leviticus 19:17-18. Try as we might, we will fail to live up to God's holy standard every single time.

Some of us may be shocked to see this mention of law. After all, aren't we now under grace? Why does James want us to think about that royal law? The example of the children of Israel in the book of Exodus is one that we should call to mind. In the book of Exodus, God miraculously delivered the Hebrew people from the bondage of slavery. And when He had called them out as His own people, He then gave them the law. They did not need to keep the law in order for God to deliver them. God delivered them out of His grace and mercy. But His grace and mercy then compelled them to follow God in holiness. They sought to follow the law in response to what God had done for them. The same is true in our lives. Jesus did not come to abolish the law, but to fulfill it (Matthew 5:17), and the promise of the new covenant is that the law of God will be written on our hearts (Jeremiah 31:31-34). We cannot keep the law in our own strength, but we do look forward to the day when that law of the kingdom will reign, and all sin and sorrow will be washed away. We await restoration and consummation of the royal law.

The command to love your neighbor seems simple at first, but once we go a little deeper, we realize that it is not as easy as it seems. At the beginning of chapter two, James focused on partiality and showed us how we are all guilty of this at times. The command to love our neighbors is perfectly personified in Jesus Himself. He came to earth and became a man—He became our neighbor. And then in sacrificial love, He laid down His life for His neighbors. So we look to Jesus as our great example of how we should love. We are to give mercy because it is what we have been given.

James words sink straight to our hearts. Partial obedience is not obedience. If you fail in just one small way, you have not kept the law and you de-serve God's righteous judgment. God knows that we will not be able to keep the law perfectly, yet still he commands us to be those who do not show partiality and extend mercy. The words are reminiscent again of Jesus' words in the sermon on the mount when He said, "Blessed are the merciful for they shall receive mercy." Jesus nor James is saying that we can earn mercy by showing mercy to others. If we could earn it, it wouldn't actually be mercy. Instead the message they are trying to show us is that when we extend mercy to others, we are revealing that we have received mercy. Extending mercy to all people shows that we understand the gospel. Because it is in Christ that mercy has been extended to us.

So James ends this section with the words, "Mercy triumphs over judgment." This is not our own human mercy; this is the mercy of God. God's mercy triumphs. The gospel triumphs. And even when we fail like He knows that we will, we find mercy at the cross that compels us to show mercy to those around us.

Partial obedience is not obedience.

1. *Read Matthew 18:21-35. What does Jesus say the law and the prophets depend on?*

2. *How does gratitude for what Jesus has done for us compel us to show mercy to other people?*

3. *How does love fulfill the law? Read Romans 13:8-14 as a cross-reference. How does love fulfill the law through Christ?*

.DAY 5.

....

Faith Works

James 2:14-18

What is the relationship between faith and works? We know salvation is by faith alone in grace alone, but what about works? These are timeless questions that often make us scratch our heads. They become extremely personal when we think about people in our lives who may say they believe in Jesus, but their life shows no evidence of transformation. James boldly addresses this difficult topic. His language is striking as he speaks boldly the truth of the gospel.

James speaks about people who say they have faith, but their life shows no works. To be clear, our works have absolutely no power to save us, but James is making the point that true faith always results in works. We cannot come to Jesus and not be changed. James is making the point that faith without works isn't faith at all. The reformers said that though we are saved by faith alone, true faith is never alone. This is the truth that James seeks to unpack for us here.

James then goes on to give an example. He speaks of a brother or sister in the church who doesn't have the money for proper clothing or daily food. This is desperate need. James fearlessly speaks to this hypothetical situation and asks what good it is if we look at a hungry and ill-clothed brother and sister and offer empty words without action. Perhaps God desires for you to be the answer to the prayers of your brothers and sisters in need. Perhaps their daily bread will come at your hand. Empty words have no power to help the needy, and empty words have no power to save. If our so-called faith consists only of empty platitudes and religious lingo it is not true faith. Jesus has the power to save us and He gives to His children a faith that is active. True faith works. True faith doesn't work as a way to earn salvation because we could never earn it. True faith works because of salvation.

The illustration James gives is just one example of a living faith, but it is one that we should pay attention to. Both the Old and New Testaments are concerned for the poor and needy, and Jesus tells us that His people are too. 1 John 3:17-18 reminds us that we should love not simply in words, but also in deeds. Matthew 25:31-34 paints a beautiful picture of why the believer must care for the needy by showing us what God does for His people. He blesses and calls His own to Himself with love, mercy, and grace. But then in Matthew 25:35-40 we see the response of the believer to what Jesus has done. Believers care for the needy, the hungry, and the oppressed. And these verses stunningly tell us that when we do that, we are not just doing it for the people in front of us, but for Jesus Himself. This truth should compel us to serve the weak and lowly among us. We do not serve others as a way to earn God's mercy, we serve because we have already been showered in mercy. Works are our response to grace.

James doesn't shy away from bold truth when he tells us that faith without works is dead. James is telling us that faith that is alone, isn't true faith at all. He gives us another hypothetical as he anticipates that some may view works as akin to a spiritual gift. They think that some have faith, and some have works, but James boldly responds saying that works are the evidence of faith.

He blesses and calls His own to Himself with love, mercy, and grace.

1   *What is the difference between true faith and dead faith?*

2   *Read Matthew 25:31-40. How does this passage shift your perspective?*

3   *In what ways can faith be evidenced in your life through works?*

" **the Father of lights, who does not change** "

JAMES 1:17

—

Every good and perfect
gift is from above, coming
down from the Father of
lights, who does not change
like shifting shadows.

Weekly Reflection JAMES 1:26 – 2:18

Paraphrase the passage from this week.

What did you observe from this week's text about God and His character?

What does the passage teach about the condition of mankind and about yourself?

How does this passage point to the gospel?

_____

_____

_____

_____

_____

_____

_____

_____

_____

How should you respond to this passage? What is the personal application?

What specific action steps can you take this week to apply the passage?

_____

_____

_____

_____

_____

_____

· DAY 1 ·

The fruit of salvation

James 2:19-24

James continues to explain the fruit of salvation. He is giving us a clear picture that true faith is always evidenced in works. He speaks directly in verse 19 when he references believing God. James' Jewish readers would have known exactly what he was talking about. He was quoting the Shema from Deuteronomy 6:4 which was one of the most important passages to the Jews and one that they recited daily. This declaration of one God and the rest of the passage stood in stark contrast to the popular polytheistic religions of the time period. This was foundational to their faith. But James is driving home an important point. Even the demons believe the Shema. The demonic powers have all the right doctrinal answers. They know that there is one God and they know what He requires. In one sense they believe, but James wants us to realize that simple intellectual assent is quite different than true faith. He uses this example to contrast for us people that say that they believe in Jesus, but their faith is not true faith at all.

James then gives two illustrations of this important point. He is going to show us two biblical characters and at first glance they couldn't be any more different from one another. He presents for us Abraham and Rahab. One is the Father of the nation of Israel and the other is identified for us as a prostitute. He first turns our attention to Abraham. The language in the passage is striking and some have even accused James and Paul of contradicting one another, but as we look closer, we will see that is not the case. Instead we will see how James and Paul present the beauty of the gospel from different angles.

We are pointed to the life of Abraham and first to something that took place in Genesis 22. In this passage, Abraham is asked to offer up his son Isaac as a sacrifice. We must be careful to think about this story in context. In Genesis 12 God had made great promises to Abraham including the promise that through his seed the whole world would be blessed. It was the promise of the Messiah. But there was one glaring problem. Abraham had no children. He was an old man and him and his wife Sarah were barren. But decades after the promise was made when Abraham was 100 years old, God kept that promise in a miraculous way and Sarah gave birth to a son. God had done the impossible, but now God was asking Abraham to sacrifice his precious only son. It was a beautiful foreshadowing of the cross. A picture that points us to how God willingly sacrificed his own Son for us. Abraham by faith journeyed up that mountain to sacrifice his son.

Genesis 15 make it clear to us that Abraham was justified by faith, and James even quotes that passage here. This happened decades before the passage found in Genesis 22. Abraham was already justified in the eyes of God, but as he lived out his faith in God, he was demonstrating that his faith was real. Verse 22 points out that his faith was completed by his works and this could also be translated as matured. Abraham was bearing the fruit of true faith. Works are the fruit of salvation, not the means of salvation. The works of the believer that flow from the transformation of redemption are an evidence of faith. These works have no power to save, but they are a demonstration that the individuals faith is true faith and not merely the intellectual assent that even the demons have. Faith without works is not faith at all.

Abraham's faith in God worked in his life in a million little ways. He wasn't a perfect man, but his justification came from the righteousness of Christ in His place. But the fruit of redemption was an evidence that he had been transformed by God's power. And as a result, he was called a friend of God. We can't do it on our own, but with the power of God working in us we can live lives in which our faith bears fruit.

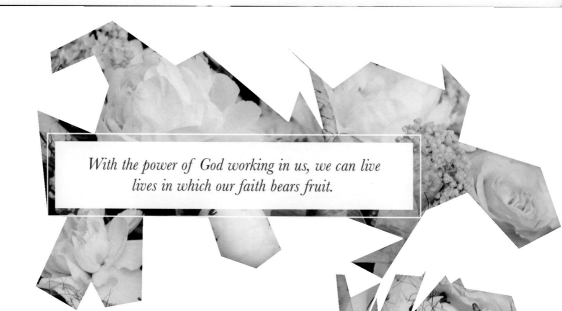

With the power of God working in us, we can live lives in which our faith bears fruit.

1) *What is the difference between the faith of salvation and the belief that the demons have?*

2) *Read Genesis 15:1-6 and record how Abraham was justified or counted as righteous.*

3) *Read Genesis 22:1-18. How was Abraham's faith demonstrated in this passage? How was God's faithfulness demonstrated in this passage?*

. DAY 2 .

the scandal of grace

James 2:24-26

God's grace is scandalous. It reaches down to sinners and pulls them from the grave of their sin to walk in resurrection life. James speaks about faith that results in action. Though these works have no power to save us, they are the evidence of our justification. And then he shows us two examples. James points us to the patriarch and the prostitute. At first glance they couldn't seem any more different. We are presented with the most revered patriarch and leader of the Jewish people. Abraham is a great leader known for his faith in God. And then we see Rahab who is identified for us as a prostitute. She was at the very bottom of the social strata and yet she is named alongside one of the greatest giants of the faith. It seems the differences between them are innumerable, and yet there is one great similarity. They both had faith that manifested itself in action. Their faith produced fruit.

So who is this Rahab? We find her story in Joshua 2 and 6. When we come to her story, the children of Israel are about to enter the promised land after years wandering in the wilderness. But in between the people of God and the promised land stood the wall of Jericho. And it was in that wall of Jericho that Rahab lived. She was a prostitute and it was likely she had not chosen that profession on her own. As a prostitute, her home was in the wall of Jericho and she ran an inn of sorts where she could entertain travelers and customers. That is exactly where we find her when the two spies come to her home. They needed to be hidden from the king and this unlikely woman would exercise great courage in being the one to hide them. In Joshua 2:11 we see her pronounce a great profession of faith in the God of Israel, and then we see her act on that faith by risking everything to hide these men.

Just a few chapters later after the walls of Jericho had come tumbling down, we see that one part of the wall was left standing, it was the home of a prostitute named Rahab who had become a child of God. But Rahab's greatest honor isn't being named alongside Abraham here in the book of James, or even being listed in the great "hall of faith" passage in Hebrews 11. No, there was a far greater honor that was bestowed on this unlikely woman. In Matthew 1 we find her name tucked amid the names of Abraham, Isaac, and Jacob. Yes. This unlikely woman would be named in the lineage of the Messiah. She was the great, great grandmother of David and part of the family tree of Jesus. This is scandalous grace. It is grace that takes an outcast and makes her a daughter.

Our faith is evidenced by our works. It was true for Isaac as he walked up the mountain willing to sacrifice his son, and it was true for Rahab as she risked everything in order to protect the spies from danger. The scandalous grace of God is so great that it not only has the power to save, but also to produce in us the fruit of sanctification. This isn't about what we bring to the table because we bring nothing but filthy rags. Instead it is about the work of the Spirit that transforms us little by little into the image of our Savior. Perhaps this is why James chooses two people who are very different as our examples because growing in godliness and bearing fruit is for every child of God. It may look different for each of us. It is going to take time. But through the power of the Spirit, all believers will grow little by little in godliness.

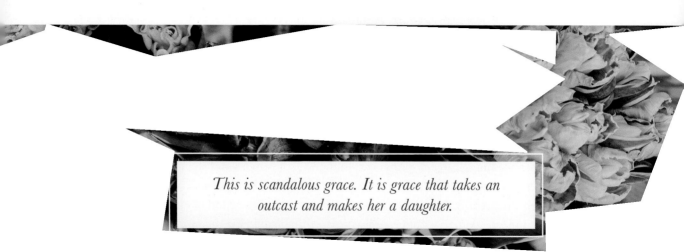

This is scandalous grace. It is grace that takes an outcast and makes her a daughter.

1. *Read Joshua 2 and Joshua 6:22-25. What do you learn about God from Rahab's story?*

2. *What are the differences between Abraham and Rahab? What are the similarities?*

3. *Why do you think James would use two very different people to prove his point?*

. DAY 3 .

the Teacher
and
the Tongue

James 3:1-2

Words are powerful and important. As we begin to study chapter 3, we will see that our words are the theme of this chapter. We should not be surprised that James has decided to dedicate so many words to the topic of our words. In James 1:18 we learned that it is by the Word of Truth that God has brought us forth in salvation. In James 1:19 we were commanded to be slow to speak. In James 1:26 we saw that the bridling of the tongue is one of James tests of true religion. James has made it clear that words and the tongue are an important topic and he will continue to develop this theme throughout the rest of the chapter.

At the start of this chapter on our words comes an intense warning to teachers. James tells us that not many should be teachers. Clearly teachers were needed, but James wants to make it clear that the role of a teacher and specifically a teacher of God's Word is a role with a weighty responsibility. Though it seems that James focuses in on those who formally teach the Word of God, the verses are applicable to all of us in some way because we all teach those around us. Whether teaching our children, a large crowd, or proclaiming who God is to our coworkers by our actions and words we are all teaching a theology lesson every day. So while these words speak to teachers directly, we would be wise to listen up.

It is interesting to think about the role of a Bible teacher in the early church. At the time that James penned these words, most people could not read and did not have a copy of the Bible. Believers were dependent on godly teachers who were diligent to teach truth to them directly from the Word of God. Though today we have stunning access to the Word of God, teachers still greatly influence our perception of the Bible.

Each of us is responsible to be wise and discerning with who we are listening to and careful to align what they say with the Word of God. And though each of us is responsible to choose our teachers diligently, James emphasizes the responsibility of the teacher to present the Word truthfully and fully. Similar warning was given in 2 Timothy 4:1-5 when Paul urged that the Word of God and sound doctrine be preached, and not simply what sounds good.

The teacher of Scripture should teach with humility and reverence. They should be keenly aware that they will give account for every word that comes from their mouth (Matthew 12:36-37). The platform of public speaking and teaching provides an opportunity for many words to be spoken, which in turn leads to many chances to speak incorrectly. The teacher should be humble with what they think they understand, and never quick to make guesses as to what a text means, but instead search out the Scriptures and humbly respond when they do not know the answer.

Verse 2 reminds us that all people stumble and sin in many different ways, but this sin of speech is a universal problem. When the apostle Paul sought to describe the depravity of man, it is no wonder that he spoke much about the words that we say in his description of our fallen condition (Romans 3:13-14). And when Isaiah came face to face with God upon His throne, it is no accident that he was aware of his unclean lips (Isaiah 6:5). James tells us if we did not struggle with sins of speech that we would be perfect. This is his way of telling us that this is a widespread problem that impacts every one of us. And though he makes some sharp statements to teachers, he does not leave any person out of his declaration of the power of words.

Sin with our words can leave us feeling hopeless in this all-inclusive sin struggle. But we need only look to our God to be given a proper perspective of words. He spoke the word into existence. He brought us forth by the Word of truth. And Jesus Himself is known as The Word (John 1:1). The hope for our fallen words is to turn our hearts to The Word.

We need only look to our God to be given
a proper perspective of words.

1. *Why do you think teachers have a great responsibility for their words?*

2. *Read John 1:1 and John 1:14. How does Jesus name being the Word, and the description of Him as full of grace and truth give perspective to the words you say?*

3. *James indicates for us that sin with our words is a universal problem. How have you seen this to be true? In what ways have others hurt you with their words? In what ways have you hurt others with your words?*

.DAY 4.

Small and Mighty

James 3:3-6

The tongue is small but mighty. James has already told us sins of words are something that we all struggle with and now he dives even deeper into the dangers and pitfalls presented by such a small part of our bodies. His descriptions remind us that we cannot be who God wants us to be if we do not grow in the area of our words. We cannot have self-control without learning to control our tongues. We cannot be holy without our words being purified.

The first two illustrations that James give show us that the tongue, though it is small, has great power to control and guide every part of our lives. James first uses the illustration of a bit in the mouth of a horse. A bit is tiny compared to the overwhelming size of a horse, and yet this great and mighty animal is guided and controlled by a small piece of metal in their mouths. The tongue is the same. It has great power over every part of us. Then James moves to another picture of the same point. He encourages us to look to the great ships and the powerful winds that they endure, and yet the thing that guides the great ships are small rudders directed by a pilot. The smallest part of the ship is the one that leads it down its path.

Our tongues are powerful though they are small. Our words may seem insignificant, but they have unmeasured influence on our lives and the lives of other people. In Matthew 12:33-35 Jesus said the words that come from our mouths, come from the overflow of our hearts. Our hearts control our words, and our words control nearly every aspect of our lives with their influence.

In his final illustration of the tongue, James turns to fire. The greatest of wildfires starts with a single flame, and the greatest of our problems so often begin with damaging words. Our words set fires of destruction that cannot easily be extinguished. Our words hold in them the power to destroy relationships and people. Proverbs 18:21 tells us that death and life are in the power of the tongue, and Proverbs 12:18 teaches us that our words can either wound or heal. James gives ample space in his short letter to this topic because as verse two reminded us, it is a topic that impacts every one of us.

The tongue can set our entire life and course on fire, and verse six says that it is set on fire by hell. The language is strong because James is making a difficult and important point. If we look closer at the word that is translated most often as hell, we learn this is the Greek word *Gehenna*. Gehenna was a location just outside Jerusalem at the time of the writing of James and the life of Christ where heaps of trash burned nonstop, night and day. James is pointing us to one of the most disgusting things that he could think of. But the picture goes even deeper than that. The location of Gehenna was known as the Valley of Himnon in the Old Testament time period and the intertestamental period. It was at this location that people sacrificed their children to the pagan false god Molech. Could there be anything more despicable than child-sacrifice? This is why Jesus likened this location to hell itself that was prepared for Satan and his demons. James is pointing us to this place of unrestrained wickedness to illustrate what we do with our words when we do not control them.

Our words have the power to destroy. And yet the gospel gives us hope for the redemption of our hearts and also of the use of our words. The mouths that so often speak critical, prideful, hurtful, cutting words can be redeemed to speak words of life and gospel-hope. Jesus who is the Word has the power to redeem our words and grow us in godliness and sanctification.

The greatest of our problems so often begin with damaging words.

1   *In what ways can the tongue control and guide us?*

2   *Read Matthew 12:33-35. What do you think Jesus meant when He said that out of the abundance of the heart the mouth speaks?*

3   *What positive or negative attitudes have you seen revealed by the words of yourself or others?*

. DAY 5 .

Taming the Tongue

James 3:7-12

Most of us are readily aware that our tongues need to be tamed. We can think back to times when our words have hurt others. We likely have all experienced a moment when words slipped from our lips and we saw hurt come across another person's face from what we said. With these things in mind, the words of James in verses 7-8 may at first seem defeating. James states that though every animal can be tamed by man, man has no power to the tongue.

We cannot tame our tongues or control our words. Our tongues are restless and unstable and constantly waiting to attack. They are full of deadly poison that wounds and kills. We are powerless to eradicate this sin that dwells deep with us. But Jesus is not. We cannot tame our tongues, but Jesus can. In our flesh we cannot make the changes needed so that our words are life-giving instead of wounding, but through the power of God, we can change. This is the hope of the gospel, that we do not have to be what we have always been. We can be changed by the power of God and the power of His Word at work in us.

James presses into the irony of the way that we use our words. Out of the same mouth we bless and praise God, and curse people who have been made in His image. We speak words of life and proclaim the greatness of God, and then we use our words to wound. You can hear James' pastoral care as he reminds us that this is not the way that things should be. How often is this true of us as well? We praise the Lord for His goodness and we spend time studying His Word, and then we use our words to criticize, gossip, or cut down the people around us who have been made in His image. This is not what God has called us to as His children.

We are pointed to nature as an example of why this should not be so. Our lips like our hearts should not be double-minded. And the words that proceed from our lips declare to those around us what is in our hearts. The real problem is not just what comes from our lips, but the sin that has taken root in our sinful hearts. We must allow God to change the sin in our hearts so that the words of our lips are changed by Him. We have no power to change ourselves, but the power of change is in Him.

So what is the answer to taming our untamable tongues? The answer is to run to the Lord who is the only one who is able to change us and change the words that come from our lips. Our words can harm those around us, but life is found in the life-giving Word of God (James 1:18). When it seems like our words hold power over us and we have no power to bring them into submission, we can remember that Jesus has defeated sin and death when he spoke, "It is finished," from the cross (John 19:30). And now He has given us a message to proclaim. The gospel has words and we are called to speak this message of life to the world around us (Romans 10:14-17).

We cannot control our words in our own strength, but as the children of God we are united to Christ and He is the one with the power to redeem our words and use them for His good and for His glory. We have no power to change ourselves, but Jesus does, and the gospel does.

We have no power to change ourselves, but Jesus does, and the gospel does.

1 *Why do you think sins with our words are something that everyone struggles with?*

2 *We have no power to tame our tongues, but God has the power.*
   How can we allow Him to change us?

3 *Paraphrase James 3:9-10.*

"
*quick to listen,
slow to speak*
"

JAMES 1:19

—

My dear brothers and sisters,
understand this: Everyone
should be quick to listen, slow
to speak, and slow to anger.

Weekly Reflection JAMES 2:19–3:12

Paraphrase the passage from this week.

What did you observe from this week's text about God and His character?

_____

_____

_____

_____

_____

_____

_____

What does the passage teach about the condition of mankind and about yourself?

_____

_____

_____

_____

_____

_____

How does this passage point to the gospel?

_____

_____

_____

_____

_____

_____

_____

_____

_____

How should you respond to this passage? What is the personal application?

What specific action steps can you take this week to apply the passage?

_____

_____

_____

_____

_____

_____

· DAY 1 ·

Two kinds
of Wisdom

James 3:13-16

James has been teaching us about some of the sins that we struggle with, and now he will set up a contrast for us. He is going to show us that there are two different kinds of wisdom, and he wants us to pay attention to his words. Wisdom is a key theme in the book of James. We saw this evidenced in one of the very first verses of this short book (James 1:5). But wisdom, knowledge, and understanding are key themes in all of the Bible. And wisdom should be evidenced by our actions.

Wisdom must begin with knowing God. We must not only have a knowledge of Him academically. We could perfectly recite gospel-truth without ever letting it transform us, but this is not what we want. We must allow the truth of the gospel to not only transform our thinking, but also to transform our hearts. In James 1:5 we learned that if we lack wisdom (and who doesn't), we can ask God for it. Wisdom comes from knowing God and His Word. True knowledge is far more than simply an understanding of the facts. Adam knew his wife Eve in the most intimate way as is the picture of the oneness of the marriage relationship. God knows His people not just in an intellectual way, but in a way that elicits deep love and affection. This is the kind of wisdom and understanding we should seek after. We seek after a knowledge of God that transforms our every thought and action — and most of all, transforms our hearts. Knowledge, understanding, and wisdom are so intertwined that we see these concepts used nearly interchangeably in the book of Proverbs (Proverbs 1:7, 2:5-6, 9:10). It is the fear, reverence, and awe of the Lord that leads us to wisdom, knowledge, and understanding.

Our actions reveal our hearts. Just as we learned that our words reveal our hearts, so do the things we do and the attitudes that we have. The wisdom of the world and the wisdom of God stand in opposition to one another. Wisdom and meekness go hand in hand because it is in understanding who God is and who we are in relationship to Him that our life comes into perspective. Meekness and humility allow us to rest.

The characteristics of this worldly wisdom are listed for us. They are bitter jealousy and selfish ambition. The descriptors placed on these words change them greatly. We can be jealous (the Greek *zelos* could also be translated as "zealous") for the glory of God and for what is good and holy. But bitter jealousy is always sinful. It is envy and covetousness. In the same way we can have ambition and aspirations that are godly. But selfish ambition is rooted in pride and sin. It may even do the right things for the wrong reasons. James tells us to not fool ourselves into thinking we are wise if these things reside in our hearts. These sinful attitudes do not come from the Lord.

These attitudes James describes as earthly, unspiritual, and demonic. They are the opposite of godly wisdom. The wisdom from God is not earthly, worldly, or human, but it is godly and holy. The wisdom from God is not unspiritual or rooted in the sinful nature of our flesh; it is rooted in the righteousness imputed to us through Jesus. The wisdom from God is not demonic or from that great enemy; it is from God Himself. This is a study of contrasts that should make us plead for God to change us into His image. And these sinful attitudes always lead to disorder and evil. This doesn't end well. Destruction will follow when these attitudes are present in the home, the church, or any area of our lives.

But there is hope for those of us that read these verses and feel the sting of conviction. We know that these attitudes all too often creep into our hearts. Instead of trying to cover these sinful attitudes, we must come to the Lord in confession and repentance knowing that He will change us. The one who has saved us also has the power to transform us.

The wisdom from God is not earthly, worldly, or human, but it is godly and holy.

1. *Wisdom is a significant theme in the book of James. What did we learn about wisdom in James 1:5? Read Proverbs 1:7, 2:5-6, and 9:10 for a deeper look at wisdom.*

2. *In what ways have you seen bitter jealousy or selfish ambition in your own life?*

3. *The fruit of the world's wisdom is the opposite of the fruit that the Spirit produces in our lives. Read Galatians 5:19-23 and list the fruits of the Spirit below.*

.DAY 2.

....

True Wisdom

James 3:17-18

True wisdom is the wisdom from above. This is the wisdom for our lives that we so desperately need. While the wisdom of the world, the flesh, and the devil is the wisdom that comes most naturally to us, the wisdom from above is the fruit of a transformed life. This should be the new normal for the child of God. This should be the fruit of one who is seeking to put sin and the flesh to death and live the new life in the power of the Spirit.

The wisdom from above is at its core rooted in humility. The wisdom that the world has to offer is one of rise, selfish ambition, and bitter jealousy. The world tells us to put self above everything else. But this is not the wisdom that comes from above. True wisdom is humble before God and before man. We are humble before God because we have tasted of the goodness of the gospel and we have recognized our deep need for Him. In turn, humility before God should produce a humility before other people. Because when we truly grasp the depth of our own depravity and the magnitude of God's mercy and grace toward us, we will be gracious and merciful to those around us. Wisdom rooted in humility produces fruit in the lives of God's children.

James lists these character traits for us, and the list bears a striking resemblance to two other prominent lists in Scripture. The first is the fruit of the Spirit that Paul listed for us in Galatians 5:22. The lists do not match identically, but the tone and essence of the passages are the same. The fruit of the Spirit and the wisdom from above should be evidences of transformation in the life of the believer. The other list that is mirrored here is a list spoken by Jesus in His longest recorded sermon. We have already seen several ways that the book of James contains echoes of Jesus' words in the Sermon on the Mount and this is another example. The wisdom from above bears a striking resemblance to the beatitudes found in Matthew 5:3-12. Perhaps as James wrote these words, he recalled the words that His brother Jesus spoke in His most famous sermon.

While the wisdom of the world is the seedbed for disorder and every evil practice, the wisdom of God is altogether different. This wisdom is pure. It is established in a foundation of a desire to please the Lord without selfish motives. It is peaceable. This is not a faulty peace where sin is ignored to make things go smoothly. Instead it is peace that stems from Jesus who is our peace (Ephesians 2:14). It is gentle. True wisdom is clothed in the meekness of Christ. It is open to reason. It is not stubborn or harsh. It is full of mercy. Because of the mercy that Christ has extended to us, we should overflow with mercy toward others. It is full of good fruits, because the life of every child of God will bear evidence of the transforming work of God in their lives. It is impartial. It does not play favorites, but instead walks in step with God's heart. It is sincere. All of these things are done not as a way to show off, make others think we are more spiritual than we are, or for any other self-serving motive. Instead these fruits of wisdom should be born out of hearts that yearn to love and serve God more each day.

Verse 16 is clear about the results of the world's wisdom. Strife, disorder, and evil always result from sin. But God's wisdom produces a harvest of righteousness. The fruit of righteousness is the result of a life rooted in humility and engulfed in the peace that the gospel brings.

The wisdom of God is altogether different.
This wisdom is pure.

Compare and contrast the characteristics of the two kinds of wisdom found in James 3:13-16.

<table>
<tr><td>WISDOM OF GOD</td><td>WISDOM OF THE WORLD</td></tr>
</table>

Read Galatians 5:22 and Matthew 5:3-12 and compile a list of all the character traits and evidences that should be present in the life of God's people.

List out 2-3 that you struggle with. In what specific ways can you seek to grow in these areas with God's help?

. DAY 3 .

....

a war within you

James 4:1-3

What causes problems in our lives? When there is strife and strained relationships, where does it come from? This is the question that James sets before us in these short verses. He sets a question before us and makes us think, but then he also gives us an answer. And it is likely that the right and true answer that James gives to us is not the answer that would have been first on our lips.

When presented with the question of what or who is the problem, we would likely fill in the blank with the people or situations that bother us the most. Certainly these are the things that are causing the strife in our lives. Yet James' answer is shockingly the opposite. He tells us that the problem is with us. We are the issue. He uses the forceful language of war to show us the depth of the problem that is set before us. He wants us to see that this is not an issue to shrug off. The source of the brokenness we find ourselves in is our own passions. These are the selfish desires that so often fill our hearts. This is our sin. And it is these sinful and selfish passions that splinter our relationships not only with other people, but with God as well.

These passions that war within us are the idols of our hearts. And this sin that we readily find ourselves in is a worship problem. Things have gotten mixed up in our hearts. We should not be surprised. This problem is not new. A quick look back to the Fall in Genesis 3 reveals that desire was cultivated in Eve's heart before she ever took a bite of that forbidden fruit. The things that we desire have the power to control us if we will let them. The problem is revealed in the New Testament as well. The apostle Paul references in Romans 1:25 how mankind exchanges the truth of God for a lie and soon we worship the creation instead of our Creator. This is what we do with our passions. We elevate the things we desire to the place of God in our lives. In essence we try to make ourselves and whatever we desire the god of our life. And this is simply disastrous.

James tells us that we covet and when we don't get what our envy desires, we murder. This is another reference to The Sermon on The Mount. We have no reason to think that James is speaking of literal murder, but in Matthew 5:21-22 we learned that the anger that rises in our hearts is the same as murder. We want what we want and when we don't get it, the world better watch out. It is no wonder that there is often strife in marriages. Two people that have their own inward passions are likely to have conflict when those passions collide. Sin is the cause of brokenness in relationships. It fractures the relationships we have with other people, but it also fractures our relationship with God.

James moves on to speaking about prayer and points out how these passions impact our prayer life and relationship with our God. Those sin-ful desires that have taken root in our hearts can cause us not to pray, and if we do pray, they can cause us to ask for the wrong things with the wrong motivations. It is possible that James is reminding us of the thing that he told us we could ask for and receive in James 1:5. But instead of asking according to the will and character of God, our passions convince us to even pray from a self-centered posture. The impact of these sinful passions is far-reaching into every aspect of our lives.

The remedy for the problem of our sinful passions is the gospel. Our hearts can be changed through the gospel in salvation and in sanctification. We must look to the cross and to our Savior who is our example of humility and sacrifice (Philippians 2:1-11). There is freedom in humility from our desire to control and the idols that so easily crop up in our hearts. And true humility is found only in the gospel and looking to the One who has humbled Himself for us.

The remedy for the problem of our sinful passions is the gospel.

1. *What are the passions, desires, idols, and sins that cause strife in your own life?*

2. *Why is it important for us to recognize the true root of the strife in our lives?*

3. *Read Philippians 2:1-11. How is Jesus our perfect example of humility? What can we learn from His example?*

.DAY 4.

Divided affections

we cannot be friends
of the world and
friends of God

James 4:4-5

James has spoken into the problems of interpersonal strife. He has pointed us to the source of strife and quarrels. But in this section, he shifts away from the problems that we cause in our relationships with other people, to the problems that we cause in our relationship with God.

He opens verse four by calling his hearers an adulterous people. In the Greek, this could be literally translated as "adulteresses." His reference is pointing us to the nation of Israel in the Old Testament. God had called the nation of Israel to be His people, but they had spurned His steadfast love and run their own way. The Old Testament speaks of God as pursuing His people like a groom pursues His bride.

Throughout the Old Testament, however, we see that the Israelites committed spiritual adultery by turning to idols (Jeremiah 3:20, Ezekiel 16, Isaiah 57:2-3,8, Hosea 1-3). They wanted the blessings that God brought, but they did not want to be faithful to Him alone. Like an adulterous spouse they cheated on God by chasing after their foolish passions. Israel's adultery was idolatry. We may be quick to think that idolatry is not a struggle for us. But we do not need to have our homes filled with idols made of gold and wood to have idols that occupy our hearts and pull for our affections.

James has likened the relationship between the believer and God to a marriage and now he likens it to friendship. The friendship that is spoken of here is not simply being an acquaintance, but it is a deep friendship of sharing life and common goals with another person. But James makes it clear to his original audience and to us as well that we cannot be friends of the world and friends of God. Those who are friends of the world, live as though they are enemies of God. Jesus has paid the price on the cross for His people to be reconciled with God. We must not now live as though we were God's enemies. Instead, we must live in light of our union with Christ and live with our affections set on Christ alone.

Verse 5 reminds us that our God is jealous over us. He has paid a high price for our ransom. He has entered into a covenant relationship with us. We have union with Christ. Now our triune God yearns jealously over the people who He has chosen, loved, and redeemed. He has put the Spirit within us as a down payment of the inheritance that we will receive (Ephesians 1:13-14). We must not dishonor the Spirit that is within us and the God who has redeemed us by chasing after the world's ideologies. We must guard our hearts against friendship with the world that sneaks in subtly, and instead pursue our Savior.

The message to us is the same as the message that the prophets gave to the adulterous people of Israel—repent and return. As children of God who have been called to be His people, we can live a life of repenting and returning. We don't always like the idea of repentance. It sounds negative when our world tells us to look only for the positive. But there is joy in repentance. There is joy in laying down our sin and letting God wash us clean. There is peace in repenting of our sin and being restored. There is grace in recognizing our need and coming humbly before Him.

As children of God who have been called to be His people, we can live a life of repenting and returning.

1) *Read Jeremiah 3:20, Ezekiel 16, Isaiah 57:2-3,8, and Hosea 1-3.*
How do these verses give you insight into the spiritual adultery of the nation of Israel?

2) *In what ways do you commit spiritual adultery or have friendship with the world?*

3) *How do you find hope for your sin in the message of the gospel?*

. DAY 5 .

He gives
more grace

James 4:6-7

James has clearly shown us the weight of our sin. He has reminded us of our weakness as his words have pierced through our heart with conviction. But he does not leave us there. Instead, he reminds us of the solution to our weakness—the abundant and overwhelming grace of our God. Our sin is great, but His grace is greater. Scripture tells us how to live, and then it tells us how we can do it. In ourselves, we have no power to live up to the standard of God's holiness, but through the power of God's Word and the power of the Spirit, we can be transformed into the image of God.

God resists the proud, but pours out His grace on the humble. As we see the message of the gospel, we learn humility. As we behold Jesus, we are molded into His example. The grace of God is poured into hearts that recognize their need of mercy and grace. We may know that salvation cannot be earned, but our tendency is to keep trying to earn God's favor. But grace is not found in earned merit. Grace is by definition unmerited favor. It cannot be earned. It cannot be attained in our own strength. It is a gift that is undeserved, but bestowed because of the love of God.

Verse 7 begins with a call to submit to God. The Greek here is *hypotasso*. This word is less about a passive act of submission, and more about an active action of willingly placing ourselves under the authority of another. It has a military connotation of willingly placing oneself under a commanding officer. God's heart for us is not that we would be forced into submission, but that we would submit to Him out of an overflow of our love and gratitude for Him. We can place ourselves under His authority with full confidence that He will do what is best for us and that His ways are always perfect.

As we submit to the Lord, we are also called to resist the devil. And as we resist, we are told that he will flee. We have an enemy who is real and deceitful. We have seen his attacks against mankind since Genesis 3, and sadly humanity is still falling for his time-tested and well-worn tricks. He seeks to deceive us. He seeks to make us question God's goodness and faithfulness to us. He seeks to make us think that we are self-sufficient and that our plans are somehow better than the sovereign plan of our almighty God. Sadly, his tactics work far too often on the people of God. But this command to resist comes with a promise that as we continually resist him, he will flee.

In sharp contrast to the command to resist the devil, we are commanded to draw near to God. And the promise of this verse is that is if we draw near to Him, He will draw near to us. We can draw near because Jesus has made it possible at the cross for us to come into the presence of God. We draw near, not in our own righteousness because we have none, but in the righteousness of Christ that has been applied to us. We draw near because in salvation we have been united with Christ. We pursue God because He has pursued us. In His initiating love He has chosen His children; our response to that love is to draw near to Him. This involves daily intentional seeking the Lord. It involves cultivating our walk with God through the reading and studying of His Word and through prayer. Drawing near to the Lord never happens accidentally. With intentional love He has sought us and now we can image Him and respond with intentional love by drawing near to Him.

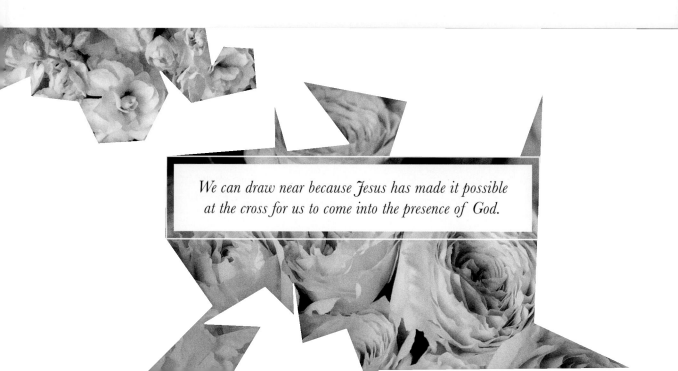

We can draw near because Jesus has made it possible at the cross for us to come into the presence of God.

1 *Paraphrase James 4:6.*

2 *What does this passage teach you about God's character?*

3 *How can you intentionally draw near to God?*

"
*if it doesn't
have works,
it is dead*
„

JAMES 2:17

—

In the same way faith,
if it doesn't have works,
is dead by itself.

Weekly Reflection JAMES 3:13–4:7

Paraphrase the passage from this week.

What did you observe from this week's text about God and His character?

What does the passage teach about the condition of mankind and about yourself?

How does this passage point to the gospel?

_____
_____
_____
_____
_____
_____
_____
_____
_____
_____

How should you respond to this passage? What is the personal application?

What specific action steps can you take this week to apply the passage?

_____
_____
_____
_____
_____
_____
_____

. DAY 1 .

. . . .

Draw Near

draw near and
He will draw near
to you

James 4:8-10

Draw near and He will draw near to you. You can almost hear James pleading with his readers in this passage. He urges them to draw near. He entreats them to turn from their sin. He begs them to humble themselves before the Lord. James wants his readers to walk in rich fellowship with God, and experience the blessings of God, but he knows that there are barriers in the way.

The words of James in this passage seem to echo the words of the Old Testament prophets who pleaded with the people of Israel to repent and return to the Lord. Throughout the prophetic books the heart of God is expressed through the inspired words of the prophets as they plead with the people to return to God. Their pleading is accompanied by a promise that if they will return, He will return (Malachi 3:7, Zechariah 1:2-3). God is sovereign and unchanging, and He is never the one that moves. In our sin, we move from Him, yet still the promise stands that if we will draw near, He will draw near to us. James speaks these words to believers. He compels them to draw near to God because God has already drawn near to us. And this is the essence of the gospel that we can freely come to Him because He has come to us. When we were dead in our sins with no strength to draw near, He made us new and drew us to Himself (Ephesians 2:1-10). Now the life of faith is one of constantly repenting and returning. We draw near to the One who has drawn us near.

In the wake of us drawing near to the Lord comes the call to repentance. As we come near to Him the posture of our hearts will be one of repentance as we see our sin and our deep need for Him alone. James tells us to cleanse our hands and purify our hearts. This combination of the changing of our actions and the changing of our hearts reminds us that both are necessary. God does not want us to simply change our actions without our hearts being transformed. And if our hearts are transformed by the power of the gospel, our actions will change. As we draw near to the Lord we will be led to repentance, and the Spirit will work in our lives.

Blessed are those who mourn. The words of Jesus in the Sermon on the Mount are echoed here in James 4:9. We must grieve over our sin. We must weep over it. We cannot experience the joy of Christ until we have first recognized our need for Christ. We live in a world that makes light of sin, and even in the church it is not uncommon for sin to be laughed about or the center of a joke. James reminds us that sin is never something to be laughed over. Instead it is something to be mourned over. Again, James words seem to echo the words of the prophets. In James 2:12-13 the Lord calls the people to weep and mourn over their sin, but the call to repentance is accompanied by a reminder of who God is. He is gracious and merciful. He is slow to anger. He is overflowing and abounding with steadfast covenant love. We mourn over our sin and we repent because He is faithful and ready to receive us.

The final words of this passage are a call to humble ourselves before the Lord so that He can exalt us. The result of beholding God is always humility. A view of God's holiness and character always reminds us of our weakness and His strength. Isaiah's response to a vision of the Lord is an example to us of the way that we should respond to the holiness of God, and that response should always be humility. The kingdom of God is an upside-down kingdom where the humble are exalted. As we behold God through His Word and see Him for who He is, we will come in humility, mourning, and repentance. Yet the grace that He freely gives to us is what calls us back to Him. It is His grace that calls us to draw near. As we behold Him, we will be humbled before Him.

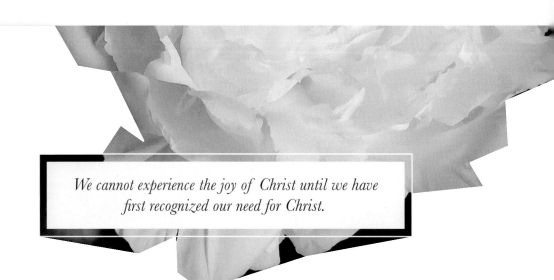

We cannot experience the joy of Christ until we have first recognized our need for Christ.

1. *The passage calls us to draw near. How do we draw near to God?*

2. *What role should repentance play in the life of the believer?*

3. *How does beholding God humble us?*

·DAY 2·

Only one
Judge

James 4:11-12

In this passage, James returns again to the issue of our speech. He spent a great deal of time teaching us about speech at the beginning of chapter 3, and now he returns to our words with the reminder of our humility before God fresh on our hearts. The placement of these words is not an accident. Our recognition of our own sin and need of humility before God changes the way that we interact with our brothers and sisters.

As we behold God and are humbled in His presence, our hearts are transformed into His image. This transformation should change our speech. Pride and sinful speech are always intertwined. Humility changes our words because we are reminded of our own need. As we grasp the mercy that has been given to us, we are enabled to show mercy to others.

James addresses speaking evil against our brothers and sisters in Christ. This can be critical speech, slander, or harsh words that are spoken to or about someone else. These sinful words show the root of pride that is present in our hearts. It shows that we have a faulty view of ourselves, and ultimately it shows that we have a faulty view of God. By passing judgment from a heart of pride, we elevate ourselves and tear others down. James says that by doing this we speak evil against the law and the faithful Judge. We try to play God when we think that we must be the ones to judge others. Our hateful and slanderous words reveal our hateful and sin-filled hearts.

By using our words to harm others, we are not fulfilling the law. This is the royal law of love that James spoke of in James 2:8. When we judge others, we set ourselves as higher than the law and ultimately, we act as if we know better than God. This is the complete opposite of the humility that God has called us to.

Instead of loving our neighbor, we often speak about them behind their backs or cut them down in our own pride. As we elevate ourselves above others, we reveal our need of humility. In the context of this passage, James is specifically dealing with our brothers and sisters in Christ. And while there are certainly times where sin does need to be addressed, it is always rooted in a spirit of humility and never from a place of pride or arrogance. When we tear down our brothers and sisters in Christ, we are declaring guilty those that Christ has made righteous through the blood of Christ.

Christians should not be known for being just like the world. We should be known for loving, encouraging, and exhorting one another. And when correction must happen and there will be times that it must, it should be done from a place of humility. Instead of critical words and gossip and slander, we should be people who earnestly pray for the needs of our brothers and sisters. We should be people who are so overwhelmed by the mercy that has been given to us that we freely show mercy to others. We should be people of humility in word and in deed.

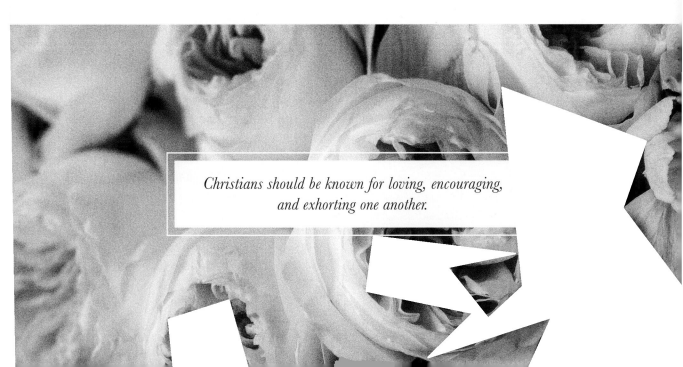

Christians should be known for loving, encouraging, and exhorting one another.

1   *How should our words flow from a heart of humility?*

2   *How have you seen slander impact your own life? Have you ever been slandered or slandered someone else?*

3   *Who are you tempted to speak critical and harsh words to or about. Take a moment to write out a prayer for them and for your attitude toward them below.*

.DAY 3.

....

the will of the Lord

James 4:13-17

The book of James confronts us. It reminds us that we need the Lord. We need Him because He is strong, and we are weak. We need Him because He is Holy, and we are sinful. We need Him because He is sovereign, and we are not. We like to think that we are in control of our lives, but there is freedom in realizing that we are not. There is freedom in humility and surrender. And this is exactly what James is teaching us in this passage.

In this passage we think through what it means to have humility before a sovereign God. James speaks to all of us in these verses as he reminds us of our tendency to make plans and think we are in control. We are being warned against a spirit of arrogance. James reminds us that we think of ourselves too highly. We do not have the power to control tomorrow or even today, but we know the One who does.

James teaches us that we must not be presumptuous. We must recognize that we cannot take even one breath without the Lord. A right understanding of God and a right understanding of ourselves will help us better understand the humility that we must have before the Lord. John Calvin famously said, "Man never attains to a true self-knowledge until he has previously contemplated the face of God and come down after such contemplation to look into himself."

A correct view of self can only be found when we have a correct view of God. As we see Him as our gracious sovereign, we begin to understand our desperate need of Him. In His mercy, God allows us to feel our need of Him.

James words here do not forbid us from making plans. These verses are not an excuse for inaction, but a call to humility. It is a call to know that every breath we take is by His grace. Every plan we make is subject to His sovereign plan. This reminder comes after many commands in this short book to action and obedience. We are reminded that we must do what God calls us to do, but we must do it in view of who God is. James is not even demanding that we use the "If the Lord Wills" phrase every time that we speak our plans. Instead he is seeking to imprint humility on our hearts.

It is common in our time for people to spend endless time thinking about what God's will is for their lives. But these verses do not push us to a life of endlessly wondering what God's will is for us. In fact, the words of verse 17 remind us that in many ways we already know what the will of God is for our lives. We do not know what will happen tomorrow, but there are some things we do know.

We know that it is God's will for us to be holy and sanctified. We know that it is God's will for us to love His Word and love our neighbors. We know that it is God's will for us to care for the outcast and the orphans. We know that it is God's will for us to serve the church. So while James has spent much of the book warning us of sins of commission, he now warns us of sins of omission. We know what God has called us to do, and how He has called us to live, and now we are responsible to live it out by His grace.

You don't have to keep it all together. Take a big sigh of relief. Our God is the One who holds all things together, and we can serve Him and trust Him with our hours, days, and years. There is great freedom in realizing that though we work and plan and seek to live our lives for the glory of God, we do it all under His sovereign care.

We know how He has called us to live, and now we are responsible to live it out by His grace.

1   *What are some things in your own life that you are tempted to think you are in control of?*

2   *How does understanding that you are powerless without Christ bring freedom?*

3   *How should this passage change the way that we think and plan for the future?*

.DAY 4.

Treasure in Heaven

wealth will fade
but God remains
ever constant

James 5:1-6

Throughout this short book, James has been straightforward and practical. It may seem nearly impossible for him to be more direct, but he certainly is in these short verses. This passage is a forceful exposition of the state of the rich that place their hope and trust in wealth. Among scholars there is some debate as to whether these verses speak of unbelievers or believers. Some of the language and historical context does seem to point to these verses addressing unbelievers, yet the warnings should be a powerful reminder for believers as well about the dangers of putting our hope in anything but the Lord.

The warning to the rich is one that calls for weeping over the judgment that is coming. James speaks to the fact that their riches have rotted, their clothing has been eaten by moths, and their silver and gold have rusted and corroded away. This is a statement about the excess that these people were living in. They had so much that their wealth was rotting like week old produce. They had so much that their clothing had been passed over and consumed by moths.

Even their gold and silver had rusted and corroded. James speaks those words to catch our attention. Gold and silver do not rust, but James is making a stunning declaration. He is saying that even the thing that seems like a secure investment is unstable and uncertain. Wealth will fade, but God remains ever constant. And He is the only One in which we can place our hope.

James speaks to the rich and says that their riches have rotted, their clothing is moth-eaten, and their gold and silver has corroded. The verbs in the Greek are found in the perfect tense. This implies emphatically that though these things have not yet taken place, they are as certain as past events. The words of these verses seem to echo those of the prophets of the Old Testament. They are a woe against the rich that trample on the poor and the vulnerable. The action described here is the antithesis of what God has called His people to be. Wealth cannot satisfy—no idol can. The only satisfaction available to our longing hearts is the satisfaction that comes through the gospel of Jesus.

James like Jesus before him is not stating that having wealth is a bad thing, but instead he is telling us that our wealth having us is a sin. The stumbling block of wealth is one that is well recorded in Scripture. Jesus Himself said that it is difficult for a rich man to enter the kingdom of God (Matthew 19:23). The warning reminds us that material wealth poses a threat to spiritual health because it gives us a false sense of security. In this way the argument of James at the beginning of chapter 5 is extremely similar to the argument at the end of chapter 4. No matter what plans we make, or what wealth we have, we must be fully convinced of the truth that we are fully dependent on the mercy of God.

The wealthy that James spoke so directly to were misusing their money. In it they found false hope. They misused it by stockpiling and not paying their employees. In verse 3, James even states that their own stockpiles of wealth will be evidence in their trial. But God is ever hearing the cries of the oppressed, the poor, and the marginalized. Verse 4 provides a beautiful reminder that God has heard the cries of the afflicted. God is referenced as the Lord of Hosts. This is a reference of God found in the Greek translation of the Old Testament and the words here are a direct quotation of Isaiah 5:9 in the LXX. The Lord of Hosts reminds us of God's might and power. It is a military designation. It likely refers to the hosts of angel armies that our God commands and could even refer to the three members of the Trinity. The connotation is that God has an army ready to go to battle for His people. He has not neglected their cries.

Even when it seemed like God was silent, He was not. Verse 6 references the condemnation and murder of the righteous person. And though this may be symbolic of the people of God, it is certainly true of the only Righteous One who is Jesus. Though He was betrayed for money, God was working and hearing the cries of His people. The crucifixion, which was the very thing that seemed the end of hope, was actually the beginning of hope for the people of God. The cross reminds us that though it seems like the wicked have all they could desire, we must not envy them. And though it seems like judgment will never come for wickedness, it is as sure as if it had already happened. And our God, though He may seem silent, hears every cry of His people.

1) *Read through the passage again and write down the things that the rich in the passage had done.*

2) *What are the things that you are tempted to place your trust in?*

3) *Why does wealth never satisfy? Where and how is true satisfaction found?*

. DAY 5 .

Be Patient

James 5:7-9

Be patient. We do not like to hear those words. We want things when we want them, and we definitely do not want to wait. Some have even joked that we should never pray for patience. Yet we come to these verses and James admonishes us to do the opposite. Not only should we pray for patience, but we must also be patient.

In light of all that James has spoken to us, he begins to conclude the book in much the same way that he began it. He calls us to patience and steadfastness. Over and over again through today's passage and the verses that follow we see that James wants this concept of patience, endurance, and steadfastness to be imprinted on our hearts. The call of the Christian life is a call to a life of patience. This is a journey of waiting and anticipating God to work in His faithful and sovereign way. We wait for Him to work and we wait for Him to come. We live our lives in expectant hope because we know that He will be faithful to His people.

James uses the illustration of a farmer who waits for his harvest. The farmer does his part and then he waits. He has no control over the timing or the fruitfulness of his crop. He plants, and then he waits. This is a clear picture of our lives. We are completely dependent on the Lord to bring the harvest. Though we are tempted to think that we have some semblance of control, we don't have an ounce. Every breath we take is a gift from God and every good thing is received from His benevolent hand.

James tells us that the fruit comes after the early and the late rains. This concept was prevalent in the Old Testament and one that his audience would have been very familiar with. In Palestine, the early rains come in October preparing the seed and the soil for the harvest. The late rains come in early Spring and saturate the seed to bring a bountiful harvest. And God is in charge of it all. From beginning to end the process is governed by His sovereign hand. Throughout the Old Testament there are references to these early and late rains, and every one of them points to the faithful God who will accomplish what He has purposed (Deuteronomy 11:14-15, Jeremiah 5:24, Hosea 6:3, Joel 2:23, Zechariah 10:1). The God who sends the rain in its season will faithfully send what is needed to prepare you and cause you to flourish.

In verse 8, the command is repeated. We must be patient. We must also establish, strengthen, or fix our hearts. The same word commonly translated as establish or strengthen is the word used in Luke 9:51 to describe how Jesus set His face or fixed His gaze to go to Jerusalem. Jesus was determined to secure our redemption. This is the way that we are called to live — with patience and hearts that are firmly fixed on the task set before us, all the while acknowledging that we are fully dependent on the Lord. The life we are called to as believers is both passive and active. The two ebb and flow together so closely that we cannot tell where one begins and the other ends. We wait because we know that it is all of God and His sovereign grace, and we work in faithfulness to Him because of that sovereign grace. This is one of James greatest themes, that a faith that is fully a gift of God is also one to which we respond with action.

Our hope is in Jesus and we know that He will restore all that is broken in the world. The story of Scripture — Creation, Fall, and Redemption will find its glorious end in Consummation. Jesus will return. The day is near and at hand, and though we do not fully understand what that means from our human perspective, we wait in hope (2 Peter 3:1-13). We wait with patience, established hearts, and unwavering confidence that God will do what He has said that He will do.

In the midst of it all, our temptation is to grumble and complain. Our temptation is to take our frustrations out on each other. Yet James urges us to be patient and to rest our hearts in the Lord while we work to build His kingdom here on earth. All the while we rest in knowing that the Lord will bring about His plan and His purposes. We rest in His grace and we wait in steadfast hope.

1. *Read James 5:7-11 marking every reference to patience or steadfastness. Below, list out the specific commands found in James 5:7-9.*

2. *Read Deuteronomy 11:14-15, Jeremiah 5:24, Hosea 6:3, Joel 2:23, and Zechariah 10:1. How does the concept of the early and latter rain encourage your heart in God's faithfulness?*

3. *How can you establish or fix your heart in this season?*

"
*the wisdom
from above
is first pure*
"

JAMES 3:17-18

—

But the wisdom from above
is first pure, then peace-loving,
gentle, compliant, full of mercy
and good fruits, unwavering,
without pretense. And the
fruit of righteousness is sown
in peace by those who
cultivate peace.

Weekly Reflection JAMES 4:8–5:9

Paraphrase the passage from this week.

What did you observe from this week's text about God and His character?

_____
_____
_____
_____
_____
_____
_____
_____

What does the passage teach about the condition of mankind and about yourself?

_____
_____
_____
_____
_____
_____
_____
_____

How does this passage point to the gospel?

How should you respond to this passage? What is the personal application?

What specific action steps can you take this week to apply the passage?

. DAY 1 .

Be steadfast

James 5:10-12

James urged us to patience in James 5:7-9, and now he comes back to the same truth. He does not want us to miss the call to faithfulness and patience. As James continues to talk about patience, he also helps us to realize that so often our patience takes place in the context of suffering. We are called to be patient and steadfast through every trial, twist, and turn that comes along our path. In many ways, James is beginning to end the book in the same way that he began. With a call to find joy in our suffering and to be steadfast through the trials of this life (James 1:2-4). James repeats these words to us because he knows that we need to hear them.

In his reminders here about patience, suffering, and steadfastness, James proceeds to give us some examples. He illustrates what it looks like to live out these concepts that can sometimes feel outside of our grasp. The first example he gives us is of the prophets of the Old Testament who were faithful and patient despite the circumstances surrounding them. As we reflect on the patience of the prophets, we could choose nearly any of them as an example here. The prophets were men who served God in spite of the situations that they found themselves in. They were faithful to proclaim the Word of God when no one would listen. They were faithful to have their lives used as illustrations. They were faithful to do what God had told them to do, even when it didn't seem to make any sense, and even when it seemed like their work wasn't doing anything. Perhaps you have felt this way. Perhaps you have wondered if the work that you are doing for the Lord matters or if anyone sees. Here James reminds us that above all, God sees. The prophets encourage us to press on in faithfulness and steadfastness.

It is here that we find another reference to the Sermon on the Mount. James says that we count those who remain steadfast as blessed. The wording is nearly identical to the wording of Matthew 5:10, where we learned that the persecuted are blessed. True blessing and true happiness are not found in the material wealth or status that the world tries to make us think is most important. Instead, true success is found in a surrendered life. True success is found in faithful service. True success is found in steadfastness and the knowledge that it is the Lord that enables us to persevere.

James then reminds us another example of patience and steadfastness in suffering as he reminds us of Job. Job faced immense suffering that is far beyond what the vast majority of us have ever experienced. He certainly had his struggles as he walked the road of suffering, but ultimately his confidence was placed in the unchanging character of God. The purpose and plan of God was revealed through the life of Job. God brought good from what seemed so bad, and we can be assured that He will do the same in our lives. Sometimes we will walk through suffering and clearly see down the road how God used it for our good and His glory. Other times, we may live our entire life unsure of why we faced a certain circumstance. But we can be assured that there was a reason. We can be confident that God will work all things for the good of His people (Romans 8:28), whether we understand during our own lives or not until the New Creation.

The Lord is compassionate and merciful. These words echo the revelation of God's character to Moses in Exodus 34:6. The character of God is steadfast and sure, and we can be confident that He will be compassionate and merciful to us as well.

The section ends with a call to stand by our word. James again references the words of Jesus in the Sermon on the Mount (Matthew 5:34-37). This verse may seem out of place, yet it echoes several of the themes that James has returned to again and again. We are called to not be double-minded. We are commanded to have a faith that works. We are commanded to be doers of the Word and not just hearers. We are commanded to have speech that honors and pleases the Lord. All of these things can be wrapped into the command to let our yes be yes and our no be no.

Our God is patient and steadfast. He is our perfect example of these things that He is calling us to be. Jesus has faced suffering before us. So we look to the example of the prophets, and of Job, and most of all we look to Jesus. And we trust that He will use whatever we are facing for His purposes.

1) *Look up the words "patient" and "steadfast" and write the definitions below. How are they similar or different?*

2) *James gives us examples of those that have patiently and steadfastly endured suffering. Is there someone in your own life that you have witnessed endure suffering with patience and steadfastness?*

3) *Why can we face suffering, trials, and difficult circumstances with patience and suffering? How do we practically do that?*

.DAY 2.
·················

Let us
pray

trust Him in the
times of suffering
and the times of joy

James 5:13-15

The call to pray is a call to rely on God fully and completely. It is an encouragement to trust Him in the times of suffering and in the times of joy. The call to prayer is a call to the life of faith that rests not in our ways, but in the ways of our sovereign God. It is a call to trust not in magical prayers, but in a good God. As James prepares to conclude this book, he calls us to pray.

So much of the teaching of James is encapsulated in verse 13. We cannot help but notice the similarity to James 1:5 when James told us that any that needed wisdom could ask of God. And just as we all are in desperate need of the wisdom of God, all of us have faced or are facing suffering of some kind. Interestingly, the answer for those that need wisdom and for those that are suffering is the same, we must pray. But then James asks if anyone is cheerful, and their need is also prayer. They are to sing praise to God which is in essence another form of prayer. In our praise and adoration of God we come before Him to thank Him for who He is. James reminds us in these verses of the necessity of prayer in the life of every child of God. Throughout the entire book James reminds us that we need God in the suffering and trials of life, and that we must not ignore the Lord when things are going well. We need Him in every moment.

While the emphasis of James 5:7-12 was on patience, the emphasis of James 5:13-18 is on prayer. But these are more connected than we might think at first glance. Patience comes through prayer. It is in patience and prayer that we wait on the Lord and trust that His ways and plans are so much better than our own. Prayer teaches us that God is our everything. We need Him. He is sufficient. In our suffering—we need Him. In our joy—we need Him. There is not a moment of our lives that we are not in deep need of His sustaining grace.

Verses 14 and 15 begin a discussion on an often debated portion of the book of James. The passage speaks of the sick calling the elders of the church to come and pray and anoint with oil. As we read this text, we should note that the focus is still on prayer in the passage. The anointing with oil is not some magical ritual; instead it is a symbol that points to a person being set apart in prayer. The elders do not have healing power; instead they pray to the One that does have the power to heal. Every prayer should be prayed in the name of the Lord and according to the will of God. We come praying for our desires and then pray, "Not my will but thine," because we know that He knows better than we do and that He will always do what is good.

In verse 15 we are told that the prayer of faith will save the sick. This verse has sadly been used to shame sick believers into thinking that their sickness is a result of their lack of faith, and that if they could just muster up enough faith, they would be healed. Instead, these words are a declaration of confidence in the sovereign plan of God. It may be that a believer will pray and be healed miraculously of their sickness. Most of us have either known of this to happen to someone that we know or at least heard of a miraculous healing that can only be attributed to God. God does work this way. But He does not always work this way. Yet even death for the believer is healing. God's plan whatever it may be is the only thing that can bring our healing. Our hope is found not in our uncertain prayers for healing, but in the healing that has already been accomplished at the cross. Every believer in Christ will one day be fully healed. Every believer in Christ will one day be raised to life just as Jesus was raised from the dead. Every believer in Christ will be fully forgiven. Our healing is not dependent on us, but on the Healer and His perfect plan. And we can be confident that His plan is always what is best for us. The prayer of faith is prayed with faith in God and His plan, not of faith in our plans.

So the exhortation for us is to pray. Pray to the God with the power to answer. Pray to the God with the wisdom to know what is best for us. Pray to the God who is our everything and know that whatever He answers is what is best for us.

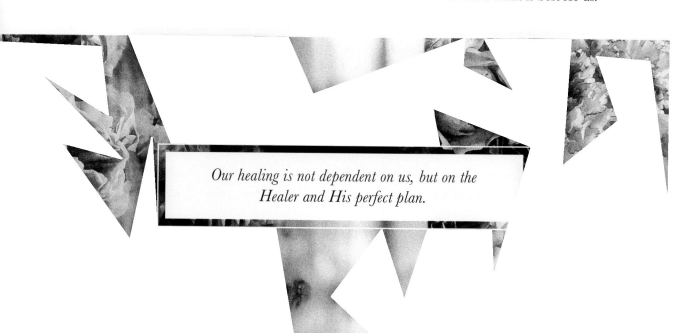

Our healing is not dependent on us, but on the Healer and His perfect plan.

① *How does this passage remind you of our need to go to God in prayer in every situation? What situations in your life do you need to pray about specifically right now?*

② *Are you more likely to pray when things are going well or when you are suffering?*

③ *Why is it comforting that God will always answer our prayers in the way that is best even when it isn't what we wanted?*

. DAY 3 .

The power of prayer

James 5:16-18

Prayer is vital and necessary. James has been showing us this throughout this passage and he continues to urge us to pray in these verses. As we read this passage, we must see that prayer is powerful because God is powerful. This isn't about us, but about Him. The power of prayer is the God to Whom we pray.

In verse 16, James urges confession of sin in the body of Christ and exhorts us to pray for one another. There should be nothing more natural than for the people of God to pray together in unity. If prayer is such a necessary part of the Christian life, and we know that it is, then it should be natural for us to pray with our spiritual family. Confession of sin to one another and prayer for each other should be normative in our church life.

The prayer of the righteous has great power. Again, it is not that prayer is some magical mantra, instead it is the power of God that is present in the prayers of His people. Our faith does not rest in the power of the words that we pray, but in the One to Whom we pray. The example that James gives us is of the prophet Elijah. His story is found in 1 Kings 17 and 18. Elijah prayed to God and it did not rain for over three years, and then he prayed at the end of that time and God sent rain. It is important for us to note that Elijah's prayers were aligned with the Word that God had spoken. Elijah prayed for what God had declared. And the prayer of Elijah was answered mightily.

This is instructional to us about how we should pray. There are many things that we know are God's will. There are things that are revealed in His Word. We know that God seeks to save the lost. We know that God desires His people to be conformed into His image. We know that God desires for His people to care for the orphan, the widow, and the oppressed. We can confidently pray these things knowing that God desires to answer them. There are other things that we do not know the answer to. We may pray about specific situations in our life that are not addressed in Scripture. We may pray for a person to be healed and we do not know whether or not it is God's will for them to be healed. In these situations, we can boldly come in prayer and make specific requests, and yet we also come humbly asking in His name and praying for His will and not our own. His will is always better than our own, and we can be confident that the way that He answers is the way that is best for us.

It is interesting to remember that these commands to pray come directly after James' teachings on patience. Prayer requires us to wait patiently before the Lord. These concepts are intrinsically connected. The life of the child of God should be one characterized by prayer and by patience. We rest in the knowledge that when we have no strength to wait in patience, He will be our strength and sustain us through every moment. We cling to the truth that when we don't know what to pray, that He will transform our prayers and our hearts. Patience and prayer exist to shape our hearts to the Lord's. In patience, we are refined to be who He wants us to be. In prayer, He does not change His will, but instead changes our hearts. Through prayer and patience, we humble ourselves before the Lord and release the anxieties that weigh us down. Throughout the book of James, we have been reminded that we need God in order to live the life that He has called us to. And through prayer we take hold of the throne of our God and are enabled to live in His power.

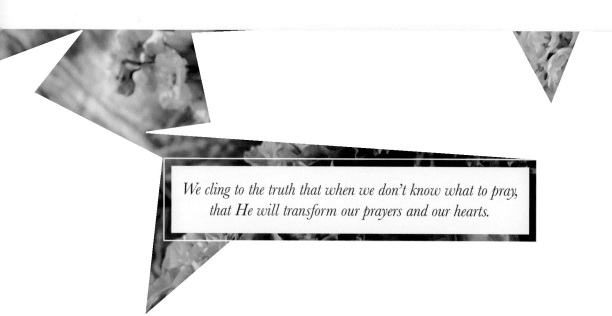

We cling to the truth that when we don't know what to pray, that He will transform our prayers and our hearts.

1. *Why do you think praying together with the people of God is important?*

2. *Read 1 Kings 17-18. What stands out to you in the story of Elijah?*

3. *How do prayer and patience work together?*

· DAY 4 ·

· · · · · · · · · · · · · · · ·

Prone to
wander

James 5:19-20

As we come to the final two verses of the book of James, it may feel like an abrupt ending to the book. But as we look closer, we can see how James uses this final command to exhort us to live out all that he has taught us in this short book. These words are James' final plea to the people of God and they encourage and exhort us to cling to the faith and encourage those around us to do the same.

In these verses, James exhorts us to do hard things. He wants us to go to those who are wandering and call them to repentance. Throughout the book of James, we have seen that we are called to a faith that works, and this final plea further enforces that thesis. This may mean that we lovingly need to have some hard conversations with those that are walking away from the Lord. James uses strong language in these verses to make a point. We know that we as humans have not power to save other people, and Scripture is clear that those who have been saved by God are eternally secure. We cannot save, but we can point people to the only One who can. Though we cannot save those around us, we must love so greatly that we seek to plead with them to return to the Lord.

We must go out seeking the lost and sharing the gospel with those who have never heard. And we must also bear our responsibility as the body of Christ to call the wandering and the struggling back to the Lord. Those who have placed their faith in Christ are eternally secure. The people of God will persevere because it is God that preserves them and enables them to do so. And yet, God often uses the avenue of community to draw us back to Himself. James reminds us that we must embrace this duty and responsibility with joy.

We have a responsibility to each other. Hebrews 13:17 reminds us that leaders in the church has a responsibility for the people that they lead. Hebrews 10:24 reminds us that we are all called to encourage one another and urge each other on to good works. This passage reinforces that truth. We are all called to watch out for each other and to do everything in our power to encourage each other along this journey.

We are called to help the wanderers return. In ourselves, we have no power to do this, but through the power of Christ in us we can encourage those around us to walk in truth. Whether a season of discouragement or a deep struggle with sin, we all face times when our hearts wander from intimacy with the Lord. This is when we need the body of Christ to encourage, exhort, and speak hard truth with grace to us. It will not always be easy to do what God has called us to do, but it will be worth it.

Throughout this book James has called us to a faith that works. The Christian life is more than just showing up on Sunday mornings and claiming the label of "Christian." The Christian life is meant to be lived out. Our faith is not one in which we simply claim to be believers, it is one in which we walk out our belief in everyday life. Faith works. It is about allowing the truth of God's Word and who He is to transform every word, thought, and action. It is about letting the message of the gospel transform us from the inside out.

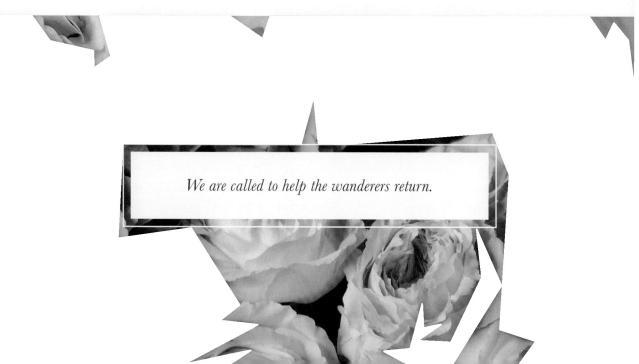

We are called to help the wanderers return.

1. *Why is active participation in church community important for what is instructed in this passage to work properly?*

2. *Read Hebrews 10:23-25. List out the things that we are commanded to do in these verses.*

3. *Who has been influential in your walk with God? How did they encourage you to follow the Lord?*

.DAY 5.

The Steadfast Life

Read The Entire Book of James

1. *Take time to read through the entire book of James again. What themes stand out to you as you read the book after having studied it?*

2. *Which verse of James would you choose as the theme verse?*

3. *Summarize the message of the book of James in a few sentences.*

" humble yourself before the Lord "

Therefore, submit to God.
Resist the devil, and he will flee
from you. Draw near to God,
and he will draw near to you.
Cleanse your hands, sinners,
and purify your hearts, you
double-minded. Be miserable
and mourn and weep. Let your
laughter be turned to mourning
and your joy to gloom. Humble
yourselves before the Lord, and
he will exalt you.

—

JAMES 4:7-10

Weekly Reflection JAMES 5:10-20

Paraphrase the passage from this week.

What did you observe from this week's text about God and His character?

What does the passage teach about the condition of mankind and about yourself?

How does this passage point to the gospel?

How should you respond to this passage? What is the personal application?

What specific action steps can you take this week to apply the passage?

Outline of the Book of James

ENCOURAGEMENT AMID TRIAL
James 1:1-18

ALLEGIANCE TO THE WORD THROUGH OBEDIENCE
James 1:19-2:12

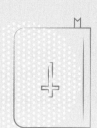

ACTIONS THAT RESULT FROM FAITH & WISDOM
James 2:13-3:12

DISCERNMENT OF GOD'S WILL & VALUES
James 4:13-5:19

— WHO WAS JAMES? —

THE HALF-BROTHER OF JESUS
—
Matthew 13:55
Mark 3:21-35
Galatians 1:19

SAW THE 5:4 *Resurrected* CHRIST

1 Corinthians 15:7

MINISTERED *with* PAUL *the* APOSTLE

Acts 12:17 | *Acts 15:14-21*

RECOGNIZED AS A PILLAR

Galatians 2:9

When James, Cephas, and John—those recognized as pillars—acknowledged the grace that had been given to me, they gave the right hand of fellowship to me and Barnabas, agreeing that we should go to the Gentiles and they to the circumcised.

James 1:1

James, a servant of God and of the Lord Jesus Christ: To the twelve tribes dispersed abroad.

Greetings.

a servant of God

And the fruit of righteousness
is sown in peace by those who
cultivate peace.

JAMES 3:18

The wicked person earns
an empty wage, but the one
who sows righteousness,
a true reward.

PROVERBS 11:18

Listen, my dear brothers and
sisters: Didn't God choose the
poor in this world to be rich in
faith and heirs of the kingdom
that he has promised to those
who love him?

JAMES 2:5

God is not partial to princes
and does not favor the rich
over the poor, for they are
all the work of his hands.

JOB 34:19

My dear brothers and sisters,
understand this: Everyone
should be quick to listen, slow
to speak, and slow to anger.

JAMES 1:19

The one who has knowledge
restrains his words, and one
who keeps a cool head is a
person of understanding.

PROVERBS 17:27

James & *Wisdom* Literature

See, we count as blessed those who have endured. You have heard of Job's endurance and have seen the outcome that the Lord brought about—the Lord is compassionate and merciful.

JAMES 5:11

After Job had prayed for his friends, the Lord restored his fortunes and doubled his previous possessions. All his brothers, sisters, and former acquaintances came to him and dined with him in his house ...

JOB 42:10-12

Yet you do not know what tomorrow will bring—what your life will be! For you are like a vapor that appears for a little while, then vanishes.

JAMES 4:14

Remember that my life is but a breath. My eye will never again see anything good.

JOB 7:7

Come now, you who say, "Today or tomorrow we will travel to such and such a city and spend a year there and do business and make a profit."

JAMES 4:13

Don't boast about tomorrow, for you don't know what a day might bring.

PROVERBS 27:1

The Sermon on the Mount & the book of James

THE POOR ARE BLESSED IN THE KINGDOM OF GOD

Blessed are the poor in spirit, for the kingdom of heaven is theirs. / Matthew 5:3

Listen, my dear brothers and sisters: Didn't God choose the poor in this world to be rich in faith and heirs of the kingdom that he has promised to those who love him? / James 2:5

THE GRIEVED ARE EXALTED IN THE KINGDOM OF GOD

Blessed are those who mourn, for they will be comforted. / Matthew 5:4

Be miserable and mourn and weep. Let your laughter be turned to mourning and your joy to gloom. Humble yourselves before the Lord, and he will exalt you. / James 4:9-10

THE MERCIFUL WILL BE SHOWN MERCY

Blessed are the merciful, for they will be shown mercy. / Matthew 5:7

If you look with favor on the one wearing the fine clothes and say, "Sit here in a good place," and yet you say to the poor person, "Stand over there," or "Sit here on the floor by my footstool?" / James 2:13

PEACE AS A FRUIT OF RIGHTEOUSNESS

Blessed are the peacemakers, for they will be called sons of God. / Matthew 5:9

And the fruit of righteousness is sown in peace by those who cultivate peace. / James 3:18

THOSE WHO EXPERIENCE TRIALS ARE BLESSED

Blessed are those who are persecuted because of righteousness, for the kingdom of heaven is theirs. Blessed are those who are persecuted because of righteousness, for the kingdom of heaven is theirs. Be glad and rejoice, because your reward is great in heaven. For that is how they persecuted the prophets who were before you. / Matthew 5:10-12

Consider it a great joy, my brothers and sisters, whenever you experience various trials. / James 1:2

HOPE AMID PERSECUTION AND TRIAL

Be glad and rejoice, because your reward is great in heaven. For that is how they persecuted the prophets who were before you. / Matthew 5:12

Brothers and sisters, take the prophets who spoke in the Lord's name as an example of suffering and patience. / James 5:10

WARNINGS AGAINST ANGER

But I tell you, everyone who is angry with his brother or sister will be subject to judgment. Whoever insults his brother or sister, will be subject to the court. Whoever says, 'You fool!' will be subject to hellfire. / Matthew 5:22

For human anger does not accomplish God's righteousness. / James 1:20

HONESTY AND INTEGRITY IN SPEECH

Again, you have heard that it was said to our ancestors, You must not break your oath, but you must keep your oaths to the Lord... Matthew 5:33-37

Above all, my brothers and sisters, do not swear, either by heaven or by earth or with any other oath. But let your "yes" mean "yes," and your "no" mean "no," so that you won't fall under judgment. / James 5:12

ADMONISHMENT TO BE GODLY

Be perfect, therefore, as your heavenly Father is perfect. / Matthew 5:48

And let endurance have its full effect, so that you may be mature and complete, lacking nothing. / James 1:4

WORTHLESS TREASURES OF EARTH

Don't store up for yourselves treasures on earth, where moth and rust destroy and where thieves break in and steal. / Matthew 6:19

Your wealth has rotted and your clothes are moth-eaten... / James 5:2-5

DO NOT BE CONCERNED WITH TOMORROW TODAY

Therefore don't worry about tomorrow, because tomorrow will worry about itself. Each day has enough trouble of its own. / Matthew 6:34

... Yet you do not know what tomorrow will bring —what your life will be! For you are like vapor that appears for a little while, then vanishes. / James 4:13-14

FIDELITY TO THE LORD

No one can serve two masters, since either he will hate one and love the other, or he will be devoted to one and despise the other. You cannot serve both God and money. / Matthew 6:24

You adulterous people! Don't you know that friendship with the world is hostility toward God? So whoever wants to be the friend of the world becomes the enemy of God. / James 4:4

THE FOLLY OF UNRIGHTEOUS JUDGMENT

Do not judge, so that you won't be judged... / Matthew 7:1-5

Don't criticize one another, brothers and sisters. Anyone who defames or judges a fellow believer defames and judges the law. If you judge the law, you are not a doer of the law but a judge... / James 4:11-12

RECEIVING FROM PRAYER

Ask, and it will be given to you. Seek, and you will find. Knock, and the door will be opened to you. / Matthew 7:7-8

You desire and do not have. You murder and covet and cannot obtain. You fight and wage war. You do not have because you do not ask... / James 4:2-3

PRAYERFULLY REQUESTING GOOD THINGS FROM THE FATHER

... If you then, who are evil, know how to give good gifts to your children, how much more will your Father in heaven give good things to those who ask him. / Matthew 7:7-11

Every good and perfect gift is from above, coming down from the Father of lights, who does not change like shifting shadows. / James 1:17

RECOGNITION BY FRUIT

You'll recognize them by their fruit. Are grapes gathered from thornbushes or figs from thistles? / Matthew 7:16

Can a fig tree produce olives, my brothers and sisters, or a grapevine produce figs? Neither can a saltwater spring yield fresh water. / James 3:12

OBEDIENCE IN ACTION TO THE WORD

Therefore, everyone who hears these words of mine and acts on them will be like a wise man who built his house on the rock... / Matthew 7:24-27

But be doers of the word and not hearers only, deceiving yourselves. / James 1:22

Thank you

FOR STUDYING GOD'S
WORD WITH US!

CONNECT WITH US:
@THEDAILYGRACECO
@KRISTINSCHMUCKER

CONTACT US:
INFO@THEDAILYGRACECO.COM

SHARE:
#THEDAILYGRACECO
#LAMPANDLIGHT

WEBSITE:
WWW.THEDAILYGRACECO.COM

———